MAGNETIC SELLING

MAGNETIC SELLING

Develop the Charm and Charisma that
Attract Customers and Maximize Sales

ROBERT W. BLY

⁴AMACOM
American Management Association
New York • Atlanta • Brussels • Chicago • Mexico City • San Francisco
Shanghai • Tokyo • Toronto • Washington, D.C.

Library of Congress Cataloging-in-Publication Data

Bly, Robert W.
    Magnetic selling : develop the charm and charisma that attract customers and
maximize sales / Robert W. Bly.
       p.   cm.
    Includes bibliographical references and index.
    ISBN 0-8144-7281-8
    1. Selling.   2. Sales promotion.   I. Title.

HF5438.25.B57   2006
658.8'2–dc22

                       2005018210

Printing number

10 9 8 7 6 5 4 3 2 1

To Sy Sperling—the greatest salesman I know

Contents

Contents

Acknowledgments

Thanks go to Bob Diforio, my agent, for his usual fine job in finding a home for this book, and to my editors, Christina Parisi, Mike Sivilli, and Niels Buessem for their patience, understanding, and editorial skill.

I'd also like to thank Ilise Benun and Linda Walker for their editorial contributions, and also thank everyone else who gave me permission to reprint or share their sales techniques and ideas in this book.

Introduction

Every business that survives does so because it sells.

—EUGENE SCHWARTZ, *BREAKTHROUGH ADVERTISING*

Have you ever walked into an auto showroom and been descended upon by a salesperson who was so pushy that you couldn't wait to get out of there?

Have you ever been served by a salesperson who was so helpful that you loved shopping at the store—and bought more than you intended— mainly because you liked talking to that salesperson?

Have you ever gotten a phone call from a telemarketer who was so robotic, annoying, and inappropriate that you hung up the phone on her in mid-sentence . . . even though you're normally too polite to interrupt people?

Have you ever eaten at a restaurant where the host, waiter, or maitre d' made you feel so welcome that you couldn't wait to get back . . . even though the food was good but not great?

The difference was not the products, services, quality, prices, terms, availability, or delivery dates: *The difference was in the personality, manner, and presentation of the two salespeople.*

In the first case, the salesperson's chemistry and actions repelled you— literally pushing you away from a product you were at least thinking of buying.

In the second case, the salesperson's personality and presentation *attracted you like a magnet*—making you want to stay longer, talk with him more, and buy what he was selling.

While most people aren't born with magnetic personalities and sales skills, those personality traits can be developed and the skills learned. That's what this book will teach you.

In *Magnetic Selling*, you will learn:

- How to exhibit the qualities that will attract people to you like a magnet
- The most common mistakes salespeople make that repel potential buyers
- How to separate genuine, qualified prospects from everyone else— and how to draw those prospects to you magnetically
- Words and phrases you can use to make people really want to do business with you
- The principle of Continuing the Conversation
- How to develop a magnetic telephone voice
- The principle of Right Timing
- How to exclude nonessential product information people consider boring or irrelevant to keep drawing them in rather than pushing them away
- The #1 thing salespeople care about that their prospects don't
- How to magnify your persuasion when closing the sale so more of your prospects place more and bigger orders with you
- How to energize customers with extraordinary service to keep them coming back to you again and again—and recommend you to almost everyone they know

When you master the principles of *Magnetic Selling*, you'll be able to:

- Close more and bigger sales, more often.
- Increase your company's sales revenues.
- Dramatically boost your personal income and wealth.

- Grow your business.
- Generate intense customer satisfaction, loyalty, repeat orders, and referrals.
- Achieve greater levels of business success and financial independence.

What's more, selling isn't just for professional salespeople. Everyone does some selling in their life, whether they know it or not, at least part of the time. *Magnetic Selling* also reveals how to apply the principles of salesmanship, charm, charisma, and a positive personality to a variety of situations at the office and at home.

At the office, you can use your newly mastered magnetic selling skills to: get a job . . . negotiate a pay raise . . . win a promotion . . . gain approval for a budget or plan . . . persuade your team to follow your lead . . . obtain the cooperation of others . . . and more.

At home, magnetic selling can help you become a more effective parent . . . improve your relationship with your spouse or significant other . . . get the things you want . . . buy a new home or car at an affordable price.

Even on small things, magnetic selling can make a difference. You can even use the principles of magnetic selling to convince others to go with you to the movie or restaurant that you choose!

I do have a favor to ask. If you have a selling technique that makes you more magnetically attractive to your prospects and customers, why not send it to me so I can share it with readers of the next edition of this book? You will receive full credit, of course.

You can reach me at:

Bob Bly
22 E. Quackenbush Avenue
Dumont, NJ 07628
Phone 201-385-1220
Fax 201-385-1138
E-mail: rwbly@bly.com
Website: www.bly.com

MAGNETIC SELLING

How to Attract Sales Leads Like a Magnet

If you would win a man to your cause, first convince him that you are his sincere friend.

—ABRAHAM LINCOLN

Do you know the twenty-five undeniable secrets of sales success—the twenty-five steps you can take to magnetically attract more prospects and close more sales—and how to apply them in your business?

The most effective sales strategies among these principles—learned in almost half a century of sales study, teaching, and experience—have now been distilled into "The 25 Principles of Magnetic Attraction," because when you follow these practices, people will want to do business with you, instead of being turned off by you as they are by so many other salespeople.

Sales professionals worldwide have closed millions of dollars in sales using these simple but powerful truths.

ATTRACTION PRINCIPLE #1:

Whether prospects buy or not is more important to you than it is to them.

The #1 thing salespeople care about that their prospects don't is making the sale. You want to close the sale because you need to make money. But the prospect doesn't care about your income or mortgage payment. She only cares about her problems, needs, and concerns. If you put her interests before your own, she will want do to business with you.

Recently my account executive at a company where I have one of my retirement accounts left the firm. The new account executive suggested some run-of-the-mill mutual funds, and—worse than the fact that they were not on any list of "top 100 funds"—they were all load funds.

When I told him I had no interest in load funds and only wanted no-load funds, his reply to me, incredibly, was "But how will I feed my family?" Why he thinks I want to pick my investments to finance his lifestyle is beyond me, but salespeople say and do things like this all the time.

Especially when business is slow or you are behind in meeting your sales quota, desperation sets in. You need the business, and so you push harder to close every sale.

When you behave in this manner, you are putting your financial self-interest—the need to earn a commission or get an order—first. It becomes very important to you to make the sale, right then and there.

Unfortunately, it's not important to the prospect. What the prospect wants is the right solution to his problem. He doesn't care about your commission, or that you need to make a mortgage payment next week, or that if you close the sale today you can meet your quota for the month . . . nor should he.

Worse, if he senses you are too eager, and pushing too hard, he will be turned off, for the following reason.

Prospects feel good about salespeople who put the customer first. They shy away from salespeople who seem more interested in closing the sale quickly than in solving the customer's problem. As J. Oliver Crom, a former CEO of Dale Carnegie, observes, "People do not want to be sold a product or service. They want to deal with people who they think have their best interests at heart and who care about them."

One way to be perceived as a salesperson who is looking out for the customer's best interest is to use this key phrase: "What would be best for you?" Especially when you're afraid that going for the close will be perceived by the prospect as you pursuing a quick commission.

For example: "We can finish the paperwork today, lock in the 5 percent discount, and get you the Deluxe model. Or we can wait, although the sale expires Saturday and we only have one more Deluxe in stock. What would be best for you?"

This way, the buyer feels she made the choice—and wasn't pressured into something that wasn't right for her.

The #1 principle of magnetic attraction for salespeople: Put the prospect's self-interest before your own. In his book *Selling Rules*, Murray Raphel tells the following story:

A man was invited by a prominent hostess to all her parties because her guests told her how much they enjoyed his company. The hostess was confused. He was no life of the party.

He was, in fact, quiet and subdued. What quality did he have that appealed to her guests that she could not see?

At her next party, the hostess introduced him to one of her guests and then, unobtrusively, remained in close proximity to hear his technique. It was very simple. After being introduced he would ask the person he just met. "Tell me about yourself . . ." And then just . . . listen.

He listened to people talk about themselves. He encouraged them to tell him about their jobs, their family, their hopes, their dreams. Where would they like to go on their next vacation? Why? For how long?

Later everyone told the hostess what a marvelous addition he was to the party.

Here's why: People who listen seem to care more, are more open-minded and concerned. Those who continually talk come across as pompous, self-centered and narrow-minded.[1]

Dale Carnegie, author of *How to Win Friends and Influence People*, said, "You can make more friends in two months by being interested in other people than you can in two years by trying to get other people interested in you."

Magnetically repellant salespeople (those who exert the opposite personality of the magnetically attractive salesperson) often rely on outdated 1960s sales training, spewing canned scripts that repulse and annoy prospects, sending them running for the door.

My wife and I were fed one of these lines recently when shopping for a mini-van.

We were in an exploratory stage, and had no reason to hurry our decision: Our old mini-van was still running, and would do so for many months. But it was becoming increasingly unreliable, and maintenance costs were getting out of control. So we were planning to upgrade soon.

When the salesperson saw that we were going to walk out of the dealership without buying, he ran after us and repeated, like a robot, a line I knew he was given in Sales Training 101: "What would it take to put you in this car today?"

Our skin crawled and we ran, he in hot pursuit. Did he ask where we were in our buying cycle—just looking or in dire need—and tailor his approach accordingly?

No. His question was clearly 100 percent motivated by his self-interest . . . his desire to get a sales commission . . . and not what might be best for us. So his personality immediately became repellant instead of attractive to us, and we responded accordingly—buying from his competitor literally across the street!

My colleague, marketing consultant Bob McCarthy, raised the question, "But wasn't the salesman doing the right thing, because he knows that if someone leaves the car lot, the sale is lost?"

Derek Scruggs, an online marketing specialist, replies:

> I've found that a better strategy is to go negative, i.e., "There's proba-
> bly no way on earth you'll buy a car today/this week/this month, is
> there?" If they agree, then you can rid yourself of any anxiety about

closing the sale. If they say no, then you can ask, "Why would you buy a car now?" and get them talking about their needs, not yours.

"The best advice I could give someone entering sales is to stop being a salesperson," says business consultant Jim Logan:

Seek to facilitate rather than sell. Focus on the needs, wants, and desires of your customers. Lead with their benefits of purchasing. Put the entire focus on them. If you offer great value and benefits, you don't need closing tricks and gimmicks. If you're really working for your customer, serving your customer, there's no need to chase them across a parking lot . . . they'll run across to you.

It should not be the salesperson's job to close everyone who walks onto the lot, but to determine which of those people are qualified prospects, and then close the maximum percentage of that group. The characteristics of what make a prospect qualified, and how to identify and attract those prospects.

Characteristics of a Good Salesperson

What makes salespeople attractive to customers? A survey of 100 buyers from the National Association of Purchasing Managers showed that what buyers consider most helpful in salespeople is knowledge, empathy, organization, responding quickly, following through, finding solutions, being prompt, working hard with a lot of energy, and being honest.

And a study from Learning International shows top-performing sales organizations are regarded highly in their industry. They consistently offer top-quality products and services that customers need and value, and conduct leading-edge research into marketplace trends and customer expectations. The study also showed that these organizations must operate at the highest levels of efficiency possible, and build lasting, mutually beneficial business relationships with customers.

In the Internet age, consumers have instant access to product information on the World Wide Web. This quick access allows them to make immediate comparisons when shopping for an item. Websites teach them what to look for in a particular product, helping them shape their "RFP" (request for proposal).

Armed with product knowledge, the consumer can craft an RFP with the exact specifications of the model, size, color, features, and options he is looking for, then go from website to website—or store to store—and comparison shop the identical item based on price.

The result is that more products are increasingly seen as commodities. The choice of which to buy, aside from price, boils down to a limited number of factors, including service, warranty, reputation of the seller, and the customer's trust in and comfort with the salesperson. Therefore, the degree to which you forge a bond of trust between you and the customer is a huge factor in determining your closing rate, average size of order, and overall sales performance.

ATTRACTION PRINCIPLE #2:

Realize that what you offer may be valuable, but it is not indispensable.

In a pinch, the prospect could live without your product or service—unless you're a surgeon about to perform a life-saving operation on a critically ill patient.

Not being a surgeon, don't exaggerate your product's benefits. Be truthful about what it can do and what it can't. For example: "This may not pay for your children's college tuition, Ms. Prospect. But it can save you hundreds of dollars in electric bills over the next several years."

You don't have to make your product look like the greatest thing since sliced bread. If you can show the prospect how she'll come out ahead by using it, that's often enough. As stockbroker Andrew Lanyi says, "The more you tell the customer you are not a guru, not a rain maker, the more credible you will be."

Marketers frequently divide products into two categories: "must-have"—those that are absolutely vital and the customer cannot live without—and "nice to have"—those that offer a benefit or enjoyment from ownership, but that the buyer could easily do without. Examples of the former include (for most of the civilized world) health care, electricity, housing, clothing, food, and automobiles.

Most products, however, fall firmly into the "nice to have" category, to varying degrees. These include books, records, magazine subscriptions, TV sets, VCRs, DVD players, video game systems, digital cameras, designer clothing, and jewelry, to name just a few.

Be honest about which category your product falls into. Do not try to convince prospects that your "nice to have" product is really a "must have." She will not be fooled. A better strategy is to show how the price you are asking for your product is a "drop in the bucket" when measured against the value-added your "nice to have" product can bring to her life.

How to Make Yourself Less Dispensable to Your Prospects

Consider this true story from Mark, a rep for a wine distributor. On one of his first sales calls, he was told by a store owner, "Your stuff doesn't sell, and I'd just as soon not have it on my shelf."

Mark went to the display and rearranged the bottles on the shelves while the owner talked to other vendors. "He screamed at me for fiddling with his shelf space, but agreed that my arrangement looked better," said Mark. The new arrangement worked exceptionally well, and the store owner ended up becoming one of Mark's best customers, inviting him to his wedding two years later.

I recently began a new hobby, purchasing a 92-gallon saltwater aquarium—an investment of more than $1,500. When selecting a store from which to buy my aquarium system, supplies, and fish, I naturally wanted a store that could provide advice, since I am a novice, and keeping saltwater fish is a complex, information-driven hobby. Just as naturally, I selected a store where the salesman was himself a hobbyist who had been keeping marine aquariums in his home for almost a decade.

So . . . are you competent? Do you understand your product, service, technology, and their applications? Is your skill set and knowledge of your market up to date? Or are you like one of those old college professors, teaching the same class for twenty or thirty years without changing a word, reading from a set of notes on pages that have yellowed with age?

During my quarter century in sales and marketing, I have observed that salespeople and business owners fall into one of four categories as far as their competence and skill in sales is concerned.

By recognizing which category you are in and taking the action steps recommended below, you can move up to the next level and significantly increase your sales performance.

A realistic assessment of your level of sales competency can also guide you as to when to listen to a sales trainer or colleague . . . and when to ignore his or her advice because your instincts tell you it is wrong.

The lowest level of sales competence is *unconscious incompetence*. You don't know what you are doing, and worse, you don't know that you don't know. You may even think you are a pretty sharp salesperson, even though to others, that is clearly not the case.

Do you think you are an okay salesperson, and blame the lack of results generated by your sales efforts always on external factors, such as bad timing, bad leads, bad customers, or bad luck? You are probably in the unconscious incompetence stage.

Recognize that you don't know what you're doing and it is hurting your business. Get help. Get a sales manager who knows more than you do. Or take a sales course or workshop.

The next stage up the ladder is *conscious incompetence*. You've recognized that the reason your sales efforts aren't working is: you don't know what you're doing.

Again, take the steps listed above. When I was at this stage as an advertising manager recently graduated from college and with only a year of work experience under my belt (instead of the considerable paunch that resides there now), I hired an experienced ad agency and leaned on them for guidance.

This strategy worked well for me and my employer. The company got better advertising than I could have produced on my own. And working with the agency accelerated my own sales education, making me a more valuable employee.

"Conscious incompetence" is better than "unconscious incompetence," because people in the former stage are amenable to guidance, while those in the latter stage are not.

My friend Jim Alexander, founder of b-to-b ad agency Alexander Sales in Grand Rapids, Michigan, once told me: "I can handle a customer who is ignorant or arrogant, but not one who is both." The unconscious incompetent is often both.

Moving higher up the ladder of sales competence, you reach the stage of *conscious competence*. You've read the books, taken the sales training, made sales calls, studied your product, and understand what works. But your experience at putting the sales techniques you've studies is limited.

That means whenever you want to create a sales presentation or proposal, you have to slow down and think about what you are doing. It doesn't come naturally.

In this stage, you should keep checklists, formulas, and swipe files (examples of successful presentations and proposals you admire) close at hand. Model your own efforts after the winners of others.

Don't try to reinvent the wheel. Observe what works and adapt it to your own product and market.

Do this enough times, and you will slowly begin to become a true master of sales. You will reach the highest level of sales competence, *unconscious competence*.

At this stage, you are selling naturally, without having to consult your checklists or reference files. The quality of your presentations is better, and it comes faster and easier.

My colleague Michael Masterson says it takes approximately 1,000 hours of practice to become really competent at sales, judo, playing the flute, or anything else. If you have expert guidance, you may be able to cut that to 500 hours.

But ultimately, you learn by doing—and doing a lot. If you are at this stage, keep doing more and more sales. When you put in 5,000 hours, you will become great, not just good, and your results will be even better.

Action step: Rank yourself using the four levels of sales competence as described here, and follow the recommendations for whatever stage you are in.

ATTRACTION PRINCIPLE #3:

Salespeople are not held in high esteem in today's society. Experts are. Why not be seen as an expert instead of a "salesperson"?

"Unfortunately, the majority of salespeople today aren't really salespeople at all," says consultant Sean Woodruff. "They offer no value and in no way attempt to differentiate themselves from the pack. It's too bad they don't realize it would take very little to listen, ask questions, listen, ask more questions, listen again, and then recommend a product. So simple yet so uncommon."

A pharmaceutical company representative selling AIDS medication comments: "Other detail men (and women) make sales presentations and push product literature on doctors. I carry a binder containing all the latest AIDS research and studies. When a doctor asks a question, I pull the relevant article or abstract out of the binder, photocopy it, and give it to him on the spot. In this way, he comes to perceive me as an information resource, not a salesman."

"You can get by on charm for about fifteen minutes, and after that, you had better know something," says Tom Hennessy (quoted in Ann Landers's syndicated column).

The previous generation of salespeople got by on "glad-handing"—being chummy with prospects, but offering no real added value. Arthur Miller paints a picture of this generation in Willie Loman as portrayed in *Death of a Salesman*.

Willie has gotten by for years because all the buyers know him. He offers no real advantage in price, quality, delivery, or style; his biggest assets are a handshake and a smile. As he ages and the older buyers retire, the younger buyers who take their place have no inter-

> est in Willy. They buy from his competitors, and he can no longer sell enough to make a living.
>
> Today to succeed in selling you have to bring something to the table: ideas, solutions, advantages—in other words, genuine added value your competition cannot offer. Otherwise, you are gone.

The more you appear to be an expert, consultant, or advisor rather than a "salesperson," the more prospects will want to do business with you. Do you think that if Dr. Phil decided to open up a private practice today, he'd have to pound the pavement looking for patients to fill his schedule?

No. And why not? Because he is a recognized expert in his field. Below are simple and easy methods you can use to position yourself as an expert in your industry, technology, or market . . . and make yourself an order of magnitude more magnetically attractive to your prospects.

Establishing Yourself as an Expert

According to Eric von Rothkirch, one problem many salespeople have is not realizing that to stand out from the crowd, and be perceived as valuable, you have to market and sell *yourself* as well as your product or service. Many people don't like the idea of taking something personal and aggrandizing it like a cheap promotion. But with a population that is increasingly technology-savvy and with an abundance of commodity products and pricing information available online, making yourself stand out through your expertise and experience has become an effective selling strategy.

So, how do you make yourself stand out from the crowd as a salesperson and position yourself as a credible, trusted expert in your product, industry, or market niche?

The process of becoming a recognized expert in your field is easy: You acquire and then selectively disseminate information about your "topic"— which may be a product, application, industry, technology, or problem—to your target market. Alan Kay, a Disney fellow at Walt Disney Imagineering Research and Development, sums up the methodology used in becoming a guru as follows: "You make progress by giving your ideas away; businesspeople haven't learned this yet."

The basic method of becoming a recognized expert is to research and gain through experience, organize, and disseminate information on your topic frequently and in a variety of formats to your target market. "Do not covet your ideas," writes Paul Arden in his book *It's Not How Good You Are, It's How Good You Want to Be* (Phaidon). "Give away everything you know and more will come back to you." To distill this to its simplest level: If you want to position yourself as a marketing consultant to audio retailers, write how-to marketing articles for their trade publication.

But that's just phase one. To truly establish yourself as a guru and set yourself ahead of the pack, you have to conduct an ongoing program of self-promotion in which information dissemination is the primary vehicle.

You can and should do a lot of other things to market and promote yourself, of course—for instance, running ads, networking, making cold calls, or sending out direct mail. But, while these generate leads, they don't do much to build your reputation.

"The great mistake of most small-business people is to imagine that their detailed knowledge of their niche market is widely dispersed," writes Gary North. "On the contrary, hardly anyone knows it. They are owners of a capital asset that others do not possess and have no easy way of possessing it."[2]

Chances are you already have substantial knowledge in one or more specialized areas. The knowledge you have gained will serve as the case of your guruship, but experience alone is not enough. You have to augment your knowledge base with further research and study.

The expert salesperson is viewed by the prospect not as a "salesman" but as a consultant or advisor. To pull this off, you need solid knowledge of your topic, but need not possess earth-shattering new data, breakthrough methodology, or unique secrets. To establish yourself as an expert, the main requisite is to present what you know—the latest thinking, proven principles, best practices—in a clear, interesting, accessible fashion.

Here are the steps in a nutshell:

1. *Writing Articles.* Writing articles for publication is the quickest and easiest way, and usually the first step, in building your guru reputation. If you want prospects to see you as an expert in their field, write articles for the trade publications they read.

"The reverence people have for the printed word is amazing," writes Edward Uhlan in *The Rogue of Publishers' Row* (Exposition Press). Simply because a person appears in print, the public assumes that he has something authoritative to say.

Getting published is not at all difficult. Trade journals, local business magazines, and association newsletters are all hungry for stories on how their readers can improve business results.

Study the publication. What type of stories do they run? Write to the editor and suggest similar stories that focus on your product, service, or method. When your article is published, mail reprints to your prospects and customers with a note, "FYI . . . thought this would interest you." They'll be interested . . . and impressed.

2. *Writing Books.* Writing one or more books is crucial to attaining guru status. In an article in *CIO* magazine about the top ten gurus in Information Technology, every one of the ten had written at least one book.

3. *Producing and Selling Information Products.* Gurus are focal points of information on a specific topic, and they enhance their reputations as experts by producing and marketing "information products" on these topics. These include audiotapes, videos, CD-ROMs, software, directories, resource guides, special reports, market research, booklets, pamphlets, and more.

4. *Publishing a Newsletter or E-Zine.* A powerful technique for building your reputation with a defined audience over a period of time is to regularly send them a newsletter, which can either be a free or paid subscription. I recommend you give your newsletter away for free, since your goal is to reach prospects, not sell newsletters.

5. *Making Speeches.* Giving keynote speeches at meetings and conventions quickly establishes your reputation as an expert.

6. *Giving Seminars.* Virtually every guru gives seminars, both to reach new prospects and to solidify his or her position as a leading expert.

Speeches are short talks, typically an hour long. Seminars, in comparison, are more comprehensive presentations ranging from a half-day to three days.

7. *Conducting a Public Relations Campaign.* Get the print and broadcast media—newspapers, magazines, radio, TV—to interview you and feature you in stories relating to your area of expertise.

8. *Using the Internet.* Another central component of establishing yourself as a guru is building a Web presence, the centerpiece of which—a website—is both an information resource and community of interest on a subject relating to your core expertise. Other e-mail marketing techniques at your disposal include banner ads, forums, chat rooms, communities of interest, online content, and discussion groups.

9. *Achieving Critical Mass.* Critical mass is the point where the business pay-off from the tasks completed in your guru action plan sustains long-term results beyond each short-term promotion.

10. *Maintaining Guru Status.* As a guru, you can't rest on your laurels. The world is changing constantly, and the leader in any field must change with it or be left far behind. You must work continually to maintain your guru status, or you may lose it.

When you read the above list, you may be thinking, "All well and good, but that's stuff my company should do. After all, they have overall responsibility for marketing this product, and a marketing department to do it. I'm just one salesperson, and my job is to sell, not to promote."

You might think so, but let me share a secret with you: in the past ten years as a freelance copywriter, I have seen an explosion in the volume of requests from salespeople who want me to help them write copy—both marketing materials for their products (including lead-generating sales letters and PowerPoint presentations) as well as PR to promote themselves as experts in their field (mainly ghostwritten articles and speeches).

Therefore, if you truly want to dominate your niche, and take your sales to the next level, you must raise your visibility and credibility to new levels— far beyond where they are now. And the best way to do that is to follow the ten-step plan above.

Where would you start? Here are three promotions you can do that aren't overly ambitious and can help you attract new prospects like a magnet: an e-newsletter, articles, and sales letters.

Write and Distribute Your Own E-Newsletter

An e-zine, or e-newsletter, is an online newsletter sent to a group of subscribers who have signed up for it because they are interested in the topic it discusses. There is typically no charge to subscribe to the e-zine. A good example is my own monthly e-zine, The Direct Response Letter, available at www.bly.com.

If you want to market your product or service over the Internet, I strongly urge you to distribute your own e-zine free to your customers and prospects. There are several reasons for doing so.

First, the e-zine allows you to keep in touch with your best customers—indeed, with all your customers—at virtually no cost. Because it's electronic, there's no printing or postage expense.

Second, by offering potential customers a free subscription to your e-zine, you can capture their e-mail address and add them to your online database. You can then market to these prospects, also at no cost.

Whether you are generating leads or direct sales, there are two ways to sell your products and services to your e-zine subscribers. One is to place small online ads in the regular issues of your e-zine. These ads are usually a hundred words or so in length, and include a link to a page on your site where the subscriber can read about and order the product.

Or, you can send stand-alone e-mail messages to your subscribers, again promoting a specific product and with a link to your site.

When you are dealing with a free e-zine (as opposed to an online newsletter, which the reader pays for), people spend just a little time reading it before they delete it with a click of the mouse. I am convinced that most subscribers do not print out the e-zine, take it home, and curl up with it on the couch later to read. Therefore, I use a quick-reading format designed to allow the subscriber to read my e-zine online right when he opens it.

In this formula, my e-zine always has between five to seven short articles. They are usually just a few paragraphs each. Every article can be read in less than a minute, so it never takes more than seven minutes to read the whole issue, though I doubt most people do. You can see the most recent issue at www.bly.com to get a feel for the length and content of these articles.

I advise against having just a headline and a one-line description of the article, with a link to the full text of the article. All this clicking forces your subscribers to do a lot of work to read your articles, and that's not what they want.

I do not use HTML; my e-zine is text only. This way it is easy and inexpensive to produce.

I don't "make a production" out of it; it's just straight type. Many readers have told me they like it this way, and that they don't like HTML e-zines, which look (a) more promotional and less informational and (b) seem to have more to read.

When preparing your text e-zine for distribution, type your copy, in a single column, in Times Roman or another easy-to-read typeface. The column width should be 60 characters, so you can set your margins at 20 and 80. However, to make sure the lines come out evenly, you must put a hard carriage return by hitting "return" at the end of each line.

There are a variety of services and software programs for distributing your e-zine as well as your e-mail marketing messages to your online database. My frequency of publication is monthly, though occasionally I do a second issue if there is major news that month.

But how can publishing an e-zine make you more in demand and bring you qualified leads? Let me give you a recent example from my own e-zine.

I gave a speech on software direct marketing. It was recorded, so I had audio cassette copies made. In my e-zine, I offered the cassette free to any subscribers involved in software marketing—potential customers for my copywriting services.

Within twenty-four hours after I distributed the e-zine, we received over 200 inquiries from marketing managers at software companies requesting the tape, many of whom needed copy written for direct mail and e-mail to promote their software.

By comparison, most lead-generating postal direct mail sent to a list of prospects average a 2 percent response. At that rate, they would have to send out 10,000 pieces of mail to generate the 200 leads I got in an hour for free.

That's what an e-zine can do for you. Once you build your subscriber list, you have an incredibly powerful marketing tool and the most valuable asset your business can own: a database of buyers with e-mail addresses and permission to mail to them at any time.

Write Articles for Fun and Fame

Just one article in a trade journal can bring a company hundreds of leads and thousands of dollars in sales. And with more than 6,000 magazines from which to choose, it's a safe bet there's at least one that could accommodate a story from your company.

Chances are that you already know which journals you'd like to approach. The magazines that cross your desk every week are strong candidates, because they're likely to deal with you and your competition.

But if you have an idea for an article that is outside your industry, or if you're just not sure which magazine would be most appropriate, here are two excellent resources: *Bacon's Publicity Checker*, from Bacon's Publishing Co., Chicago; and *Writer's Market*, from Writer's Digest Books, Cincinnati.

Bacon's is the bible of the public relations industry. It lists thousands of magazines and newsletters according to business or industry category, and also provides an alphabetical index. Besides giving the basics of magazine titles, addresses, phone numbers, and editor's names, *Bacon's* notes circulation and the types of articles published by each journal.

Writer's Market, by comparison, lists fewer publications, but describes their editorial requirements in far greater detail. Since *Writer's Market* is published primarily to help freelance writers find suitable markets for their work, it is more helpful than *Bacon's* when it comes to finding a home for a full-length feature story. If you are not familiar with a magazine that sounds as if it may be appropriate for your article, be sure to read a few issues before contacting an editor there.

Many trade journals will send a sample issue and set of editorial guidelines to prospective authors upon request. These can provide valuable clues as to style, format, and appropriate topics. They often tell how to contact the magazine, give hints on writing an article, describe the manuscript review process, and discuss any payment/reprint arrangements.

How to Write a Sales Letter

Direct mail is one of the most effective methods of generating large quantities of high-quality sales leads. Aside from public relations and postcard decks, few promotional methods can even come close to matching direct mail's effectiveness for lead generation.

A good lead-generating direct-mail letter will generate response rates between 1 and 5 percent—and sometimes higher—when mailed cold to rented mailing lists or a directory of prospect names. This response rate produces quality leads with a genuine and serious interest in your product or service—or at least in the problem your product or service solves. It can be achieved using copy with a strong sales appeal and an attractive offer that is free and without obligation.

Can response rates be higher? Yes. Some lead-generating mailings have achieved response rates of 10 to 50 percent or more, although this is rare. Response rates are generally two to five times higher when mailing to existing customers versus cold mailings to rented prospects lists.

Response rates can also increase when offering expensive free gifts or other "bribes" to prospects in return for their reply. The more costly and desirable the bribe, the more inquiries produced. But when prospects respond just for the bribe rather than a genuine interest in the product or service, conversion of leads to sales becomes poor. With lead generation, you must always balance quantity with quality of inquiries.

The most effective format for lead-generating direct mail seems to be a one- or two-page letter in an envelope with a business reply card and perhaps one insert, such as a brochure, flyer, or article reprint.

Self-mailers can also be effective. The most successful self-mailer format for lead generation is the tri-fold. This is made by taking a piece of paper

EXHIBIT 1-1. SAMPLE SALES LETTER FOLLOWING THE AIDA FORMULA.

Bob Bly
Copywriter/Consultant/Seminar Leader

22 East Quackenbush Avenue, Dumont, NJ 07628 • Phone: (201) 385-1220 • Fax: (201) 385-1138
e-mail: rwbly@bly.com • website: www.bly.com

Dear Marketing Professional:

"It's hard to find a copywriter who can handle business-to-business, industrial, and high-tech accounts," a prospect told me over the phone today, "especially for brochures, direct mail, Web sites, and other long-copy assignments."

Do you have that same problem?

If so, please complete and mail the enclosed reply card and I'll send you a free information kit describing a service that can help.

As a freelance copywriter specializing in business-to-business marketing, I've written hundreds of successful ads, sales letters, direct mail packages, Web pages, e-mail marketing campaigns, brochures, data sheets, annual reports, feature articles, press releases, newsletters, and audiovisual scripts for clients all over the country.

But my information kit will give you the full story.

You'll receive a comprehensive "WELCOME" letter that tells all about my copywriting service—who I work for, what I can do for you, how we can work together.

You'll also get my client list (I've written copy for more than 100 corporations and agencies) . . . client testimonials . . . biographical background . . . samples of work I've done in your field . . . a fee schedule listing what I charge for ads, brochures, and other assignments . . . helpful article reprints on copywriting and marketing . . . even an order form you can use to put me to work for you.

Whether you have an immediate project, a future need, or are just curious, I urge you to send for this information kit. It's free . . . there's no obligation . . . and you'll like having a proven copywriting resource on file—someone you can call on whenever you need him.

From experience, I've learned that the best time to evaluate a copywriter and take a look at his work is before you need him, not when a project deadline comes crashing around the corner. You want to feel comfortable about a writer and his capabilities in advance . . . so when a project does come up, you know who to call.

Why not mail back the reply card TODAY, while it is still handy? I'll rush your free information kit as soon as I hear from you.

Regards,

Bob Bly

P.S. Need an immediate quote on a copywriting project? Call me at (201) 385-1220. There is no charge for a cost estimate. And no obligation to buy.

and folding it twice horizontally so you form three sections (the same way you fold a business letter for insertion into a No. 10 business envelope).

To write a persuasive sales letter, use the famous "AIDA" formula. AIDA stands for Attention, Interest, Desire, and Action—a sequence of psychological reactions that happen in the mind of the reader as he is sold on your idea. Briefly, here's how it works. (See Exhibit 1-1.)

First, the letter gets the reader's *attention* with a hard-hitting lead paragraph that goes straight to the point or offers an element of intrigue.

Then, the letter hooks the reader's *interest*. The hook is often a clear statement of the reader's problems, needs, or wants. For example, if you are writing to a customer who received damaged goods, acknowledge the problem and then offer a solution.

Next, create *desire*. Your letter is an offer of something: a service, a product, goodwill, an agreement, a contract, a compromise, a consultation, a meeting, a demonstration, an assessment, an evaluation. Tell the reader how he or she will benefit from your offering. That creates a demand for your product.

Finally, call for *action*. Ask for the order, the signature, the appointment, the donation, the assignment.

Of course, formulas have their limitations. And you can't force fit every letter or memo into the AIDA framework. Short interoffice memos, for example, seldom require this degree of persuasiveness.

But when you're faced with more sophisticated writing tasks—a memo to motivate the sales force, a mailer to bring in orders, a letter to collect bad debts—AIDA can help. Get attention. Hook the reader's interest. Create a desire. Ask for action. And your letters will get better results.

Notes

1. Murray Raphel, *Selling Rules* (Atlantic City: Raphel Marketing, 2001), p. 5.
2. Gary North, *Remnant Review*, April 20, 2001, p. 5.

Words and Phrases That Get People to Want to Do Business with You

People do not want to be sold a product or service. They want to deal with people who they think have their interests or who care about them.

—J. OLIVER CROM, CEO, DALE CARNEGIE

Words are powerful. The words you say to prospects can attract or repel them.

For instance, the word "buy" repels prospects, because it means spending money. Instead of saying, "When you buy this product," say, "When you own this product." The prospect wants to envision himself owning the product, so owning magnetically attracts him.

Similarly, don't use the term "the price" or "the cost" when talking about money. Say "the investment." We don't like cost, but we do like investments.

When talking about price, express the cost in terms that make it seem low. For instance, the Mayo Clinic publishes a health newsletter that costs $27 a year for twelve monthly issues.

But the price $27 never appears on their website. Instead, the order page for subscriptions tells us to make "just 3 payments of $9." The publisher correctly recognizes that consumer health newsletters have a low price point, and is presenting the price in a manner calculated to minimize price resistance.

Make Your Prospect an Offer She Can't Refuse

Prospects are magnetically attracted to great offers—offers so fantastic they seem difficult to believe. Offers that seem so generous, they'd be fools not to accept them.

What makes for an irresistible offer? Ideally, you show the price you are asking is a mere drop in the bucket compared to the value the buyer will get from owning the product.

According to Mark Joyner in his book *The Irresistible Offer* (John Wiley & Sons, 2005):

> *The Irresistible Offer is an identity-building offer central to a product, service, or company where the believable return on investment is communicated so clearly and efficiently that it's immediately apparent you'd have to be a fool to pass it up. The Irresistible Offer cuts through all the noise and clutter. It creates an itch that the buyer has to scratch. Such an offer makes doing business with you so easy and obviously beneficial that you stand out clearly from the crowd. People remember you. People can't move quickly enough to give you their money. The Irresistible Offer sparks the customer's imagination and creates an urgent, gotta-have-it-now, buying frenzy.* [1]

So, how do you convince the prospect that your offer is truly irresistible—and that indeed your price is a mere drop in the bucket compared to all the value they will receive?

Here are a few suggestions:

1. *Make the prospect relieved to hear how little you are charging.* Do this by stating higher prices for other services or products first, then giving your

price, which is less. For instance, if you are selling reading specs, mention that laser eye surgery is $1,000, new eyeglasses can run $300 at an optician's, but your buy-by-mail reading specs are just $19.95. If you are selling an options trading course on video, first mention your $1 million minimum private managed accounts . . . your $5,000 seminars . . . by the time you get to the videos, the prospect will actually be relieved that they are only $299.

2. *Make an apples-to-oranges comparison.* Don't compare your subscription newsletter to another newsletter; compare it to another information resource, such as private consultation or expensive training. Promotions for Georgetown's American Speaker compare the $297 price to the $5,000 a top speechwriter would charge to write just one speech. Leeb's Index Options Alert notes that the $2,950 it charges for its options trading fax service is like paying a 2.95 percent fee on a $100,000 managed options account—and that it's actually lower than the total fee such a managed account would charge.

3. *Spread out the payments.* Rodale and Franklin Mint are well aware of the sales-closing benefits of offering several smaller payments vs. one large lump sum. One publisher of financial fax advisory services costing thousands of dollars found that offering subscriptions on a quarterly basis both reduced sticker shock and increased sales. If yours is an Internet service, consider offering it for so much a month (billed to the customer's credit card) rather than a big annual subscription for which they must write a large check. After all, which sounds better—"$19.95 a month" or "$240 for one year of service"?

4. *State the price in terms that make it seem smallest.* Even if you want full payment up front, state the price in terms that make it seem smaller. A $197 annual service, for instance, delivers a set of benefits all year long for just 54 cents a day—less than the price of a hamburger.

5. *Value the component parts.* If you are selling an options trading course for $299, list the individual elements and show that the retail prices of each (videos, workbook, telephone hotline, website access) add up to much more than $299—therefore the course buyer is getting a great deal.

Even better: Position one or two of the product elements as premiums the buyer can keep even if he returns the product or cancels the subscription. Offering "keeper" premiums usually increases response. Example: Instead of selling your 8-cassette audio album for $79, say it is a 6-cassette album for $79, and position the other two cassettes as premiums.

6. *Add an element that cannot easily be priced by the buyer.* Loose-leaf services, for instance, face a built-in resistance from the buyer: "Why is it X dollars if it's just a book?" Supplements help differentiate from regular books, but publishers have found it even more effective to include a CD-ROM with the notebook. The CD-ROM is perceived as a high-value item with indeterminate retail price (software on CD-ROM can cost anywhere from $19 to $499), so it destroys the "book to book" comparison between loose-leafs sold via direct marketing and ordinary books sold in bookstores.

7. *Show the value or return in comparison to the price.* Demonstrate that the fee you charge is a drop in the bucket compared to the value your product adds or the returns it generates. If your consulting service helps buyers pass regulatory audits, talk about the cost of failing such an audit—fines, penalties, even facilities shutdowns. If your seminar on energy efficiency in buildings cuts heating and cooling costs 10 to 20 percent a year, the prospect with a $10,000 fuel bill for his commercial facility will save $1,000 to $2,000 this year and every year—more than justifying your $199 public seminar fee.

8. *Find a solution with your pocket calculator.* With intelligent manipulation, you can almost always make the numbers come out in support of your selling proposition. Example: A high-priced trading advisory specializes in aggressive trades with profits of around 20 to 30 percent with average holding periods of less than a month. The challenge: Overcome resistance to paying a big price for modest-sounding returns. Solution: Dramatize the profits the subscriber can make with numerous quick trades. Remind prospects, "If you could earn 5 percent each month for the next ten years, a mere $10,000 investment would compound to a whopping $3.4 million. At 10 percent, it would be an almost unimaginable $912 million!"

9. *Pre-empt the price objection.* Most sales presentations for expensive products build desire and perceived value, then reveal price once the customer is sold. An opposite approach is to state price up front and use the exclusivity of a big number to weed out nonprospects. For example: "This

service is for serious investors only. It costs $2,500 a year. If that price scares you, this is not for you."

An element of exclusivity and snob appeal is at work here. Also, the more you tell someone they do not qualify, the more they will insist they do and want your offer. The classic example is Hank Burnett's famous letter for the Admiral Bird Society's fund-raising expedition. The second paragraph states: "It will cost you $10,000 and about 26 days of your time. Frankly, you will endure some discomfort, and may even face some danger."

ATTRACTION PRINCIPLE #4:

Make it easy to buy. Make it pleasant. And make it risk-free.

Make it easy: Accept all methods of payment (cash, money orders, checks, credit cards, PayPal, bill me); have flexible terms; do not require extensive paperwork from the customer; keep long hours; allow prospects to purchase even when you are not open (e.g., use an 800 number service to take inbound phone orders or permit ordering online).

Make it pleasant: Retrain, move, or dismiss any customer contact people with unpleasant personalities.

Make it risk free: For a service, tell the customer, "If you are not happy, we will redo the job at our expense." For a product, tell the customer he may return it within 30, 60, or 90 days for a full refund if not 100 percent satisfied.

Sears was built on this simple principle, and the Sears empire was launched with an unassuming newspaper ad that proclaimed in the headline, "Send no money now." Standard policy today, but a revolutionary idea in its time.

Years ago, a salesman for a software reseller was trying to get the business of a large corporation. The purchasing manager told him, "I would place my business with you, but we are so busy, I don't have time to generate the purchase orders for each piece of software, and the corporation does not allow me to issue a blanket purchase order for software. So I let our individual users purchase their own software directly, even though we prefer for it to go through the purchasing department."

The salesman responded, "Give me a stack of blank purchase orders. When you have an order, call me and tell me what you need; I will fill out the purchase orders for you, and fax it for your signature." This solved the prospect's problem, and the purchasing manager began ordering all of his company's software from the salesman.

Understand What Consumers Really Want

Marketing expert Russ von Hoelscher insists that people want to be loved, appreciated, and admired more than anything. They also want things like power, creativity, beauty, success, and freedom. At the same time, people want to have more money; advance their careers; have a secure future; and have more time off, good health, control, and prestige.

If your sales efforts are to be successful, you must tap into one of these fundamental human desires. If you do not give people what they want, but only give them what they need or what you think they need or want, your poor results will immediately identify your failure to pinpoint and speak to the buyer's true desires.

Copywriter Herschell Gordon Lewis says the four great motivators of our time are fear, exclusivity, guilt, and greed. Each suggests a broad range of human motivations and attitudes that can be tapped into through advertising. Take fear as an example.

Some of the things people fear are:

- Getting old
- Pain
- Humiliation
- Loss of hair
- Money worries
- Being happy
- Death

- Loss of control
- Radiation
- Toxic waste
- Pollution
- Flying
- Public speaking
- Traffic accidents
- Not being successful
- Not achieving one's dreams
- Having to live according to the dictates of other people
- Taking risks
- The unknown

This list could have been much, much longer. You could add many fears of your own. Others share your fears. A group of people sharing a common fear represents a prime target market for a specific product or service that addresses that fear.

Robert Collier says the "prime motives of human action" are love, gain, duty, pride, self-indulgence, and self-preservation. Of these, says Collier, love is always the strongest motive: "There are certain prime human emotions with which the thoughts of all of us are occupied a goodly part of the time. Tie it up to the thing you have to offer, and you are sure of prospects' interest."

Joe Karbo writes that the four basic human motivators are: Reincarnation (or the hope that in some way part of you will live forever), Recognition, Romance, and Reward (material possessions and money).

Researchers at Yale University[2] found that the following words are the twelve most persuasive in the English language:

1. You
2. Money
3. Love
4. New

5. Discovery

6. Proven

7. Guarantee

8. Easy

9. Safety

10. Results

11. Save

12. Health

New Jersey-based copywriter Sandy Aptecker provides the following list as an example of products and services and the desires they fulfill: [3]

Product/Service	Basic Emotional Longings/Desires Fulfilled
Skin care/cosmetics	Desire to be beautiful, young
Insurance	Desire for security, protection
Bank credit cards	Desire for status, power
Self-improvement programs	Desire to be smart, superior
Business seminars	Desire for knowledge, success
Travel clubs	Desire for adventure, to save
Cellular telephones	Desire to be elite, exclusive
Financial products	Desire for money, success
Collectibles	Desire to acquire, to be important
Children's toys	Desire for superior progeny
Auto clubs	Desire to avoid disaster
Charities, fundraisers	Desire to nurture others
Subscriptions	Desire to be entertained, smart
Computers/software	Desire to be competitive, save time
Vacation property	Desire for shelter, to be elite
Physical fitness	Desire for health, longevity, beauty

Tap into Guilt, Exclusivity, and Fear

Guilt is defined as a feeling of responsibility for wrongdoing. Pull the guilt trigger to make your prospects feel bad about failing to take action. You say: "Miss this chance and you may never forgive yourself." Although guilt is most often in fundraising, it can still be effectively used in other selling situations.

Another emotion you can profitably tap into is exclusivity, or snob appeal. Just as we all want to gain something of worth, we also want to feel like someone of worth, someone special. We crave importance.

Usually, that means being part of something with value. That may include a school, a special society, powerful political groups, a club, or a user group. A hint of exclusivity can be triggered by using the word "invitation." Consider these two phrases from North Light Book Club: "This special trial membership is for artists who want to keep learning and growing . . ." and "Just use the enclosed Invitation card to let us know which book you'd like FREE. . . ."

In essence, when you sell on exclusivity, you tell the prospect: "Remember, if you act now, you'll be joining the elite!" In a sense, you flatter the buyer. You kiss up to him by making him feel important. Here's an example from American Express: "Quite frankly, the American Express Card is not for everyone. And not everyone who applies for card membership is approved."

Although greed, exclusivity, and guilt are strong motivators, fear may well be the most powerful. "Greed, Guilt, and Exclusivity are all Herculean as selling arguments," said Herschell Lewis, "but Fear is the strongest, because it's the one motivator that can cause the reader to lose sleep."

To incorporate fear into your arsenal of sales tactics, you need to tell the prospect about pain and loss. Prospects will continue in pain unless they call you or accept your offer. Or you tell them what they may lose by delaying to act.

To make fear work in selling situations, you must be sincere, specific, and believable. In other words, don't just say, "Prices will go up soon." Instead, say, "On August 1, prices will go up to $29.95."

Don't just say, "Act now and we'll send you a free gift." Say: "If you respond by Dec. 15, we will send you a free PC cleaning kit." If your supply really is limited, then say it. But say it with sincerity—and in a credible manner. For example: "Only 112 kits are left. Our success has been greater than all our expectations. Once gone, they are gone forever."

And remember to be careful when using these motivators. If you pressure too much before the prospect is ready, you may lose a sale.

PROSPECT REPELLANT #1:

Pressuring the prospect to take the next step in the buying process before she is ready.

Almost universally, prospects hate sales pressure. And attempting to get a prospect to purchase before she is ready is always a pressure situation that, in most instances, is likely to drive the prospect away rather than convince her to change her mind and buy now.

Two alternatives to "What would it take to put you in this car today?" that can accelerate the prospect's buying decision in certain situations are: "I'm betting there's nothing that could get you to buy a car today, is there?" and "I know you may not be looking to buy a car today, but there's something I do want you to know about . . ." and then give a compelling reason why the prospect might indeed want to at least consider making a purchase earlier than intended, such as a clearance sale or limited availability of a special feature or offer.

If there is a legitimate reason why the prospect should buy today instead of wait, a sincere salesperson will be able to—and should— make the reason clear in an honest and enthusiastic way.

On the other hand, if there is no real reason why the prospect would be better off buying now instead of waiting, and the desire to rush the sale is only driven by the salesperson's eagerness to earn a commission, the prospect is sure to pick up on this vibe—no matter how good an "actor" you are—and be magnetically repulsed and pushed away.

Notes

1. Mark Joyner, *The Irresistible Offer* (Hoboken, N.J.: John Wiley & Sons, 2005).
2. Frederick Brown, "Marketing Strategies for the Growing Business," *U.S. Small Business Administration*, 1991, p. 40.
3. Sandy Aptecker, personal communication.

How to Become Magnetically Attractive to Prospects by Asking Them Questions and Really Listening to the Answers

*The most important secret of salesmanship is to find out
what the other fellow wants, then help him find the
best way to get it.*

—FRANK BETTGER, *HOW I RAISED MYSELF FROM FAILURE TO SUCCESS IN SELLING*

One of the most powerful techniques for becoming magnetically attractive is to put the interest of others ahead of your own. You do this by talking about what interests them, not what interests you. The only way to know what interests them is to ask questions and listen to the answers.

This chapter gives you a set of questions you can use to demonstrate genuine interest in the other person and create a conversation they will want to participate in. It also shows you how to really listen to the answer, so that you are responsive to your customer's needs, wants, and desires.

Qualify the Prospect by Asking Questions About MAD (Money, Authority, Desire)

The goal of qualifying is to give you a better than 50 percent chance of closing the sale. My qualification process focuses on getting the qualification information from the prospect. To get information, you have to ask questions.

Good qualification questions are centered on three probing areas, which I refer to as MAD—money, authority, and desire. Qualifying your leads will affect your success in sales more than anything else. The purpose of asking these questions is to find out if the prospect is qualified—that is, has the money, authority, and desire to buy what you are selling.

Money

Money is the first question to be answered. If the prospect does not have a way to pay for what you are offering, why would you be working on a specific deal? A prospect without money may have you occupied for months and prevent you from working on sales opportunities with real potential.

As a proactive salesperson, you need to be asking two questions concerning money. First, "What is the process for obtaining a budget for a decision like this?" And second, "What is the process for making a decision?"

ATTRACTION PRINCIPLE #5:

Prospects are magnetically attracted to salespeople who seem willing and able to work within their budget.

When you quote a price without having the slightest idea whether it's even in the ballpark as far as the prospect's budget is concerned, you risk quoting a price that is simply unacceptable to them.

Conversely, prospects are attracted to vendors who work to make their products and services affordable (within the buyer's budget), rather than try to sell them the most expensive item in their product line, because it has the highest commission.

Your chances of closing increase astronomically if your price quotation is within the prospect's budget. The best way to find the budget is to ask: "Do you have a budget for this purchase?"

Notice we did not say, "What is your budget?", which causes many prospects to bristle if you ask them. Instead, we asked a simple, nonthreatening question: "Do you HAVE a budget for this purchase?"

About half of prospects will answer "yes." If they answer "yes," ask: "Would you mind sharing with me what your budget is?"

About half will tell you, so you can quote accordingly. For instance, if the budget is $10,000, forget about pushing your $20,000 system on the prospect, even if (a) you feel it is the best solution to their problems and (b) it gives you the nicest commission.

You can offer them the $10,000 solution, but if you have a $9,000 system, that's even better: When prospects give you a budget, you increase your chances of closing the sale if your quote is slightly less than (about 10 percent under) the upper end of their budget.

What about the prospect who answers "No, I don't have a budget" when you ask them "Do you have a budget?"?

Instead of giving up on finding out their budget, ask the following next: "Do you at least have a dollar figure in mind of what you'd like it to cost you?"

Many prospects who do not have a formal budget for acquisition of your product will, when asked this question, provide a rough dollar range, e.g., "Well, I'd like to spend around $2,000 but I could go as high as $4,000." This would tell you that a $3,000 quote might win you their business while a $6,000 quote would be less likely to do so.

Now let's move on to the next scenario, which is that the prospect won't tell you what her budget is:

Prospects are magnetically attracted to salespeople who seem to have price flexibility.

But other times, the prospect won't tell you their budget or give any indication of what they want to pay. "I don't have a budget," she will say, "you tell me what it will cost."

How do you quote price "blind" (not knowing what the prospect wants to or can afford to spend) without being told "your price is too high" after you do so?

One strategy is to quote a range of three options: one low-end, one high-end, and one in the middle. That way you're more likely to come up with an estimate the prospect will accept.

When the choices are complicated, it helps to present the three options in writing. On your estimate, literally label the three options "good, better, and best."

My experience is that when you do this, the majority of prospects choose the mid-price option, "better." Even though the "good" option is priced lower, the prospects avoid it because most people don't want the bottom of the line package.

A smaller percentage will select the most expensive of the three choices, "best." But offering "best" has another benefit: it makes the prospect think the "better" option he has chosen is more of a bargain.

Prospects are attracted to salespeople who seem genuinely interested in helping them save money and get a bargain, while at the same time getting them good value for their money. They are turned off by salespeople who seem determined to extract every last dollar from the buyer for the sale.

Giving a prospect a choice can work in your favor, as long as the choice is simple and there are not too many options. The choice of three price ranges—good, better, best—gives the prospect some leeway without over-complicating the decision-making process.

Authority

Does the prospect you are speaking with have the *authority* to place an order with you? Or are there other decision makers that must sign off on the purchase order? The best way to ascertain this is to ask directly, "Who else must be involved in the approval process for this purchase?" Three additional questions that need to be answered are: "What is the implementation date?" "What are the steps in the buying process?" "What are the decision criteria?"

Desire

"Desire" refers to the intensity with which the prospect longs to own the product. You can pick up on this through verbal and visual clues. For instance, if a prospect leans toward you, listening intently as you show or describe the product, that type of body language indicates strong desire for ownership.

Is the prospect merely in an exploratory or research phase? Or does he have an immediate need or *desire* for your product? The best way to determine whether there is a real and immediate need is to establish whether there is a deadline, or date, by which the product must be implemented. If there is not, then the prospect is merely exploring options, and your chances of closing are much less.

Nothing kills a sale like a maybe. The implementation date is when prospects want their order on their desk or when they are going to start using your product or service. The date the contract is signed is secondary compared with the date they have what you sold them.

Prospects place importance on implementation date more than any other date in the buying process for a variety of reasons, including:

- They promised their boss something would change.
- There is a customer timeline involved.
- A schedule must be met.
- There is political pressure on something that your good or service is a part of.

All qualified deals will have an implementation date. But salespeople usually know this specific implementation date in less than 50 percent of their current prospecting forecast.

There are several reasons for this. To begin with, salespeople are focused on the selling process, and do not know about the prospect's buying process. They don't think like a buyer, and therefore focus on selling. And they don't bother to ask about the implementation date, assuming it is always ASAP (as soon as possible).

Even when you know the specific implementation date, your job of qualifying the lead is not done yet. What the implementation date does not do is tell you how the prospect is going to buy. It does not give you the steps in the buying process the buyer is going to go through, or in what direction the buyer is going to buy in. So you must ask: "What are the steps in the buying process?"

Salespeople sell forward, but buyers buy backward. Salespeople are trained to think of a next step, than the one after that, and so on, all the way until a close. This is good thinking. However, next-step selling must be based on the prospect's buying cycle, not on the seller's cycle.

Think about it. When was the last time you purchased anything of some importance? You bought it backward. For example, your last car: The lease on my car is running out this date, so I need to do something about that soon. Last vacation: We have to go on vacation the week of July 10, since that is the only week all the kids are free.

What are the reasons buyers buy? A prospect's buying decision comes down to five criteria. A decision to buy a good or service ends up focusing on:

1. Features and benefits
2. Quality
3. Support or ease of use
4. Cost
5. Image

A *feature* is something the product is or has; a *benefit* is what it does for the customer. In sales presentations, demonstrate features/benefits and the value they provide. Stress the benefits, not just list hundreds of features and hope the prospect can sort them out and pick a few good ones.

The prospect's interest in *quality* may vary, so you must ask questions to determine the level of quality the customer desires. Some customers are content with good but not great quality: in other words, quality adequate to meet the need, but no more than that. Others want the best quality money can buy.

Support deals with the service you will be getting from the selling organization. Buyers want to feel they will be taken care of and can maximize their value.

Your product or service must address the *cost* issue. How much does the customer want to spend to solve his problem? Does he want a Rolls Royce, Cadillac, or Chevy solution? And is he willing to pay for it?

Image refers to the reputation and credibility of the seller. How important is it to the prospect that you are financially stable and will be here to support him in 10 or 20 years from now? Or that you will even show up to finish the job once you cash the deposit check?

According to Vince Gupta:

Salesmanship is about relationships and building trust. Effective sellers have a head start on a trusting relationship when they can quickly show a prospect that they know something about their situation and their needs and are eager to learn more. The more efficiently salespeople can identify the right customers and then learn more about their needs, the more quickly their sales figures will rise. [1]

PROSPECT REPELLANT #2:

Not asking questions.

Not asking questions goes hand in hand with making assumptions. Both are turn-offs. When you ask questions, you demonstrate interest in the prospect and his problems, not just in your sale and commission.

> And, by asking questions, you get the information you need to offer real solutions to the prospect's problems. Not just canned goods.

If sales professionals are trained so well in communication skills, why is it that many people dislike interacting with them? From the perfume consultant trying to lure you into trying a sample in the cosmetics aisle, to the manufacturer's representative calling on a corporate vice-president, many of those in sales have garnered an unfavorable reputation of being aggressive and overbearing.

Asking questions is a productive way to begin the relationship you hope to build with your contact. By identifying and researching everything you can about your customer, you'll know who it is you're seeking to establish a professional relationship with.

For example:

- "Why do you want to change your payroll processing system?"
- "How have you worked with companies like ours in the past?"
- "When do you anticipate moving your information to this new database?"
- "Where do you plan to use this product?"
- "Who will be involved in the transition phase of this plan?"
- "What do you see is the most immediate change to be made?"

Unfortunately, instead of taking the time to ask these important questions, many sales representatives would rather pull out the company's brochure and begin reading from it or pointing to its pictures and charts.

Yes, you may have a great service. And yes, your new widget maker may increase your customer's financial bottom line. However, beginning your presentation with a sales chant of all the great things your product or service can do will simply glaze over your customer's eyes or get you shown quickly to the door.

In short, the telephone call you make or the meeting you set up is not about you or your company. It should be about the wants, problems, and concerns of your customer.

By failing to focus on her needs and asking in-depth questions, you will not only ruin the rapport you've begun. But you'll be identified as someone who is more concerned about his sales commission—instead of being known as the business partner who is looking to begin and continue a long-term, win-win partnership for both parties.

How to Improve Your Listening Skills

The success of our sales activities depends largely on how well we listen. Studies show that we spend about 80 percent of our waking hours communicating, and at least 45 percent of that time listening.

But although listening is so critical in our daily lives, it is taught and studied far less than the other three basic communications skills: reading, writing, and speaking. Much of the trouble we have communicating with others is because of poor listening skills.

The good news is that listening efficiency can be improved by understanding the steps involved in the listening process and by following these basic guidelines.

Most people are not great listeners. Many years ago, Sperry (now Uni-Sys) did a survey and found that 85 percent of all people questioned rated themselves average or less in listening ability. Fewer than 5 percent rated themselves either superior or excellent.

You can come up with a pretty good idea of where you fall in this spectrum by thinking about your relationships with the people in your life: your boss, colleagues, subordinates, customers, best friend, and spouse.

If asked, what would they say about how well you listen? Do you often misunderstand requests, or only vaguely remember what people have said to you? If so, you may need to improve your listening skills.

The first step is to understand the four steps of the listening process:

1. *Hearing* is the first step in the process. At this stage, you simply pay attention to make sure you have heard the message. If your customer

says, "I need the drawings on my desk by Friday noon," and you can repeat the sentence, then you have heard her.

2. The second step is *interpretation*. Failure to interpret the speaker's words correctly frequently leads to misunderstanding. People sometimes interpret words differently because of varying experience, knowledge, vocabulary, culture, background, and attitudes.

   A good speaker uses tone of voice, facial expressions, and mannerisms to help make the message clear to the listener. For instance, if your customer speaks loudly, frowns, and puts her hands on her hips, you know she is probably upset and angry.

3. During the third step, *evaluation*, you decide what to do with the information you have received. For example, when listening to a sales pitch, you have two options: You choose either to believe or to disbelieve the salesperson. The judgments you make in the evaluation stage are a crucial part of the listening process.

4. The final step is *responding* to what you have heard. This is a verbal or visual response that lets the speaker know whether you have gotten the message and what your reaction is. When you tell the salesperson that you want to place an order, you are showing that you have heard and believe his message.

When it comes to listening, many of us are guilty of at least some bad habits. For example:

- Instead of listening, do you think about what you're going to say next while the other person is still talking? Salespeople, thinking we know the answers and that customers do not, often tune out what the buyer is saying.

- Are you easily distracted by the speaker's mannerisms or by what is going on around you?

- Do you frequently interrupt people before they have finished talking? Engineers, who value facts rather than feelings, often interrupt to set the listener straight, not realizing that the listener has a need to express himself fully, whether he is right or wrong.

- Do you drift off into daydreams because you are sure you know what the speaker is going to say?

All of these habits can hinder our listening ability. Contrary to popular notion, listening is not a passive activity. It requires full concentration and active involvement and is, in fact, hard work. The following tips can help you become a better listener:

1. *Don't talk. Listen.* Studies show that job applicants are more likely to make a favorable impression and get a job offer when they let the interviewer do most of the talking. This demonstrates that people appreciate a good listener more than they do a good talker.

Why is this so? Because people want a chance to get their own ideas and opinions across. A good listener lets them do it. If you interrupt the speaker or put limitations on your listening time, the speaker will get the impression that you're not interested in what he is saying—even if you are. So be courteous and give the speaker your full attention.

This technique can help you win friends, supporters, and sales. Says top salesman Frank Bettger, "I no longer worry about being a brilliant conversationalist. I simply try to be a good listener. I notice that people who do that are usually welcome wherever they go."

2. *Don't jump to conclusions.* Many people tune out a speaker when they think they have the gist of his conversation or know what he's trying to say next. Assumptions can be dangerous. Maybe the speaker is not following the same train of thought that you are, or is not planning to make the point you think he is. If you don't listen, you may miss the real point the speaker is trying to get across.

3. *Listen "between the lines."* Concentrate on what is not being said as well as what is being said. Remember, a lot of clues to meaning come from the speaker's tone of voice, facial expressions, and gestures. People don't always say what they mean, but their body language is usually an accurate indication of their attitude and emotional state.

4. *Ask questions.* If you are not sure of what the speaker is saying, ask. It's perfectly acceptable to say, "Do you mean . . . ?"or "Did I understand

you to say . . . ?" It's also a good idea to repeat what the speaker has said in your own words to confirm that you have understood him correctly.

5. *Don't let yourself be distracted by the environment—or by the speaker's idiosyncrasies.* It's sometimes difficult to overlook a strong accent, a twitch, sexist language, a fly buzzing around the speaker's head, and similar distractions. But paying too much attention to these distributions can break your concentration and make you miss the point of the conversation.

If outside commotion is a problem, try to position yourself away from it. Make eye contact with the speaker, and force yourself to focus on the message, not the environment.

6. *Keep an open mind.* Don't just listen for statements that back up your own opinions and support your beliefs, or for certain parts that interest you. The point of listening, after all, is to gain new information.

Be willing to listen to someone else's point of view and ideas. A subject that may seem boring or trivial at first can turn out to be fascinating, if you listen with an open mind.

7. *Take advantage of your brain power.* On the average, you can think four times faster than the listener can talk. So, when listening, use this extra brainpower to evaluate what has been said and summarize the central ideas in your own mind.

That way, you'll be better prepared to answer any questions or criticisms the speaker poses, and you'll be able to discuss the topic much more effectively.

8. *Provide feedback.* Make eye contact with the speaker. Show him you understand his talk by nodding your head, maintaining an upright posture, and, if appropriate, interjecting an occasional comment such as "I see" or "That's interesting" or "Really." The speaker will appreciate your interest and feel that you are really listening.

Motivation is an essential key to becoming a good listener. Think how your ears perk up if someone says, "Let me tell you how pleased I am with that report you did," or "I'm going to reorganize the department, and you are in line for a promotion."

To get the most out of a meeting, speech, or conversation, go in with a positive attitude. Say to yourself, "What can I learn from this to make me more valuable in my industry and to my company?" You might be surprised at what you can learn, even from routine meetings and bull sessions at the water fountain.

PROSPECT REPELLANT #3:

Not listening.

It's a cliché, but it's absolutely true: you have two ears and one mouth. So you should listen twice as much as you talk. The late Howard Shenson, a marketing consultant, said that in meetings with prospects, salespeople should listen 80 percent of the time, and talk only 20 percent of the time.

To listen, you must develop two characteristics: first, patience. You can't be in a rush to say your piece. Let the prospect say his first.

Second, you need to develop a genuine interest in the prospect and his needs, problems, and concerns. Are you really interested in the prospect? Or do you just say you are, but really, you don't care about them?

When I am not focused on the prospect and am putting myself first, I take a deep breath and think about this: how will my product or service make a positive difference in the prospect's life?

I also think about what a shame it would be if the prospect did not get these benefits, because I failed to communicate these unique benefits to him. After that, my conversation becomes much more focused and caring, and therefore, more effective.

Notes

1. Vince Gupta, "Qualify Leads Before Making the Pitch," *DM News*, May 2, 2005, p. 20.
2. Frank Bettger, *How I Raised Myself from Failure to Success in Selling* (Englewood Cliffs, N.J.: Prentice Hall, 1947).

Secrets of Successful Cold Calling

The quality of a person's life is in direct proportion to his
commitment to excellence, regardless of his field of endeavor.

—VINCE LOMBARDI

Many people think that to be successful in cold call sales, you must be as persistent as a pit bull and never take "no" for an answer—no matter what.

But in today's highly competitive sales market, these techniques, left unrefined, will get you nothing but a loud slamming of the receiver in your ear. Because, let's face it, the term "telemarketer" doesn't evoke the image of someone you'll want to drop whatever you're doing to talk to.

Just as with the car salesman who begins his spiel with "What will it take to sell you a car today?"—no one wants to hear an opening line cliché or an obviously rehearsed speech. You're setting yourself up for failure if you don't take the time to understand the attitude of the person you're calling—or examine the reason behind why you're in the cold calling business to begin with.

Most will agree, cold calling is the most universally despised aspect of sales—even those in sales don't carry such a high opinion of the technique. As one salesman says, "I call up strangers, say my spiel, and if they don't like it, I move on to the next number on my list."

That might work fine for a person doing a temporary job. But who could possibly thrive in a long-term sales career under such terms?

When many people hear the words "cold call" they think of a room full of people sitting in a generic-looking room, dialing number after number off a sheet of paper in order to make their call quota for the hour.

We think of the telemarketers as high-pressure salespersons out to make a few bucks or, at the very worst, as con artists eager to swindle a poor unsuspecting soul. After all, who would want to make a career out of calling strangers at dinnertime—or an executive during a busy workday—to sell replacement windows or a bigger ad in the local business directory?

Negative connotations such as these can run strong in the minds of not only your potential customer, but also on the mind of someone who doesn't feel comfortable doing cold call sales to begin with.

So how do you, the cold call salesperson, get past these negative impressions and really feel good about what you do for a living? The first step is in building or boosting your self-confidence. According to Donald Trump, decision makers want to know they can totally put their trust in you to produce the desired results. They develop this trust by seeing your confidence.

In his book, *The Way to the Top: The Best Business Advice I Ever Received*, Trump says confidence is shown in several ways. Decision makers look for someone who speaks with authority, and who conveys a commanding presence by appearance, posture, eye contact, and body language—and by showing a track record of ongoing successes.

Think about the last time you were at a large group gathering—like a party. As you looked around the room at the clusters of people talking and laughing together, there always seemed to be one person in every group who had command of the conversation. What was his magic formula that held the others' attention?

Confidence and charisma are certainly a large part of it; likeability, manners, attitude, and appearance are also in the mix of ingredients. What could this person teach you about sales? A lot. "But I'm sitting in a small office," you say. "No one sees me as I do my cold calling—I'm on the phone. How can I do anything when I don't see my customer face-to-face?"

To be successful in cold call sales, you must believe in your product or service. Otherwise, you'll be quickly intimidated, shy, apologetic, and yes, even possibly embarrassed for yourself and what you're selling. You'll make excuses. Falter in your delivery.

And if you don't believe in what you're selling, how can you possibly expect anyone else to listen, ask questions, and show sincere interest in what it is you're saying? In short, your selling skills depend, in large part, on your level of self-confidence—and the belief you have in the product or service you represent.

PROSPECT REPELLANT #4:

Selling a product or service you don't believe in and would not buy yourself.

There are two reasons salespeople don't believe in and don't buy the products they themselves are selling: Either they are not part of the target market for that product, or they know their company's product is not as good as competing products.

If you are not part of the target market for what you are selling, you are at an enormous disadvantage, because your knowledge of this market is secondhand and inadequate.

Sure, you can do research, and in some instances, that's the best you can do to fill in the gaps in your understanding of the buyer's core complex. For instance, if you are a pharmaceutical rep selling to doctors, it's unlikely that you will get an M.D. just to understand your customers better (if you do become an M.D., you're not likely to continue working as a pharmaceutical rep).

On the other hand, if you sell to a target market that you can get closer to, either by becoming one of them or participating in some of their activities, you should. This will give you greater understanding of and empathy with your prospects, and they in turn will sense this in you and be magnetically attracted to it.

Master copywriter Clayton Makepeace advises anyone who sells, "Make yourself have experiences similar to the prospect's." For instance, if you are selling stock market advice, you need to know how investors think and feel about the market. The best way to do this is to invest a significant amount of your own money in the stock market—significant enough that when the market turns bearish, you lose sleep at night worrying about your portfolio taking a nosedive.

Similarly, if you are selling toys, children's clothing, or learning programs for children, you should become a parent assuming that fits in with your lifestyle and goals. Having your own children will empower you to be much more in tune with your customers, who are themselves parents.

When you say, "I remember when my kids wore this design," you create an instant bond with the prospect, because you identify yourself as a fellow parent. Conversely, if the prospect asks, "Did your children play with this?" and you are forced to answer, "I don't have children," your credibility diminishes and you put distance between yourself and the prospect, weakening whatever connection you had already established.

Just like a dog sniffing out its prey, most astute customers can immediately sense whether or not you believe in yourself and your product or service. That initial belief can set up the beginning of a positive relationship or end it in a matter of minutes.

PROSPECT REPELLANT #5:

Talking too fast.

As John Brentlinger observes in his *The Little Blue Book of Selling*: "When a prospect hears a salesperson talking fast, they think that the salesperson has something to hide, something to sneak through, and the prospect begins to lose trust in the salesperson. Whether or not this assessment by the prospect is accurate is not the question. It is the perception of the prospect, and we all know that to the prospect, perception is reality. The end result is that the prospect does not feel confident buying from a fast talker. So, they don't buy.

> "Even if your parents talk fast, if you were taught to talk fast in high school and college, and even if you won awards in speech class for being the fastest talker, it does not matter. You must talk slow enough and deliberate enough so that the prospect trusts you, understands you, and comprehends everything you say. Listen to your prospects. Three out of four of them talk slowly and deliberately. Do the same for them."[1]
>
> So stop talking fast. More prospects will trust you, more prospects will buy from you, and you will sell more and make more.

Try to match the speed, tone, and urgency of the person you are talking with. If you are speaking to the one person out of four who is a fast talker, speed up the conversation a bit; if you talk to a harried, pressured executive in a slow, lazy drawl, he will lose patience.

Further, develop the chameleon-like knack for matching the prospect's mood, tone, and personality. When I talk to a prospect who is street-smart, I allow my middle-class origins to shine through (I grew up in Paterson, New Jersey, not the most urbane or bucolic of towns). When talking to a prospect who is analytical, I let my analytic side take over (I am a chemical engineer by training).

You can't be like everyone, so don't be a fake. At the same time, all of us have multiple interests and facets to our personality. When dealing with others in business, practice the art of "mirroring," which means showing those facets—aspects of temperament, belief, and attitude—that most closely align with the prospect.

Why? For this simple reason: People like doing business with those whom they perceive are most like themselves. An elitist dandy will most likely buy from another elitist dandy, while a farmer is more comfortable with a salesperson who has some experience in farming.

Also be aware of your volume when speaking. "A soft voice can be used to manipulate others, or it can indicate a person who himself is easily swayed," write Jo-Allan Dimitrius and Mark Mazzarella in their book, *Reading People*. "While a low tone may initially suggest that the speaker lacks confidence and assertiveness, don't be fooled. A soft voice may well reflect calm self-assurance: the speaker feels no need to dominate a conversation."

Cultivate Self-Confidence

Self-confidence can be learned. Everyone experiences times when they doubt themselves and their ability to successfully conduct and close a sale. But when it becomes an ongoing battle, you must ask yourself, is this career right for me? If the answer is still yes, you must learn to increase your self-confidence through practice and learning more affirmative behaviors.

Very few of us bound out of bed first thing in the morning ready to take on (or sell to) the world. But once we've downed that first cup of coffee and we begin our day, our sense of self and the confidence we carry with us comes to the forefront. Many successful sales professionals have a personal routine that gets the self-confidence going and has them eager to pick up the phone.

Here are a few examples of what might work for you:

● *Dress the part.* Although no one's going to know you're making phone calls before shaving and you're lounging in your sweats—you know! If you're working from home or a hotel room out of town, make it a routine to get as ready as you would as if you'd be heading to your office. By dressing the part, you're more apt to behave and present yourself in a professional manner. If you've got a very important call to make—put on your best clothes. When you feel your best, chances are you'll do your best.

● *Eliminate all distractions other than the task at hand.* If a personal problem needs to be addressed, try to handle it before mixing it up with your work life. If you've got business concerns on your mind, consider organizing your workday activities so that everything possible can be handled so as not to interfere with your concentration. It is important to present a positive demeanor to others—whether you're in a face-to-face meeting or speaking over the telephone.

● *Do your homework.* Like your mother always told you, be prepared. There's nothing worse than having your potential customer ask you a question and you can't answer it because you can't find your notes. Organize your notes and use them. Think through as many possible scenarios as possible and be ready with a thorough reply.

If you're caught off guard, you can always compliment your customer on an excellent question and tell her you'll get back with the answer within a short amount of time—and then do so. If you don't plan ahead, you'll find yourself muttering "uh" and "um" and "hold on just one second" while the clock ticks, you shuffle papers, and the customer waits. Not a good thing, as Martha Stewart would say.

Before you make your first call of the day, have a satisfying, healthy meal, exercise a bit to get the blood flowing and the mind sharp, and then do a short—perhaps five or ten minutes—mental run-through of your day, or a mental rehearsal of that first important phone call.

To get yourself in the confident mood required for cold calling, try a bit of positive self-talk. If you think this is silly or isn't important—think again. How did you respond the last time someone gave you a compliment? Did you shrug it off or reply that it was nothing?

Negativity is everywhere we go—even expected of us if we don't want to appear conceited or bold. Why are you so willing to believe the negatives over the positives in your life? In thinking over your upcoming cold calls, ask yourself this—if you don't think you deserve the sale, do you really think the customer is going to disagree?

Use every opportunity to give yourself credit for a job well done. When a particular transaction goes well, relive it several times during the day and just before you go to sleep at night. Congratulate yourself on doing a good job. It's okay to feel proud of your accomplishments. Experiencing the joys of success empowers you to continue to believe in yourself and do a good job.

Some people find that practicing how you're going to approach your customer in front of a mirror helps. Find a space that's private and where you won't be interrupted. As you go through your rehearsal, pay particular attention to not just your tone of voice, but your facial expression and your body movements.

Are you sitting up straight in your chair or slumping over your desk with your chin in your hand and the telephone receiver balanced on your shoulder? When you're finished practicing, tell yourself no one can do this job any better than you. The more specific you can be, the better it is. And the more you practice your confidence-building routines, the more your self-esteem will grow. You might feel self-conscious when you start to practice these new behaviors but once your self-confidence grows, those feelings will disappear.

Visualize Success

In today's competitive environment it's not enough to want success—you have to create it. By visualizing yourself in a winning situation, you will achieve that success. Again, find a quiet spot and put yourself in a comfortable position. Remember—no ringing phones or intrusive family members. This is your time.

For example, if you're a nonprofit fundraiser, picture yourself putting on such a powerful presentation that your prospective donors have no alternative but to contribute goods, services, or a large monetary donation. Look closely at the imaginary scene. What are you wearing? What kind of room are you in? How is the seating arranged? Can you see your audience asking questions? Picture yourself providing thorough answers.

Feel how at-home you are because you have the right answers to their eager questions. Look around—they're nodding their heads in agreement. After you've finished the presentation, the decision makers come forward to shake your hand. They're saying things like, "What a great job! We've never been that moved to contribute to such a worthy cause. In fact, we'd like to talk to you about doubling our donation from last year."

Notice how you're standing up straighter, making eye contact, and smiling. You've done everything right and your goal has been accomplished. As you end this visualization exercise, take note of the relaxed, happy feelings you're experiencing. Do a form of this exercise every day—in some situations, you'll be cold calling and other times you're imagining meeting your customers in person.

What will happen in your vision will become your reality if you dedicate yourself to this discipline. By imagining—and believing in—yourself, you'll achieve what you've set out to do. Because you've practiced so often, the actual phone call will be easy to do—because you've done it so many times before in your head.

Warm Up Your Cold Call

Even if your career involves cold call sales, how do you feel when you're being solicited either at home or at the office? Chances are, you dislike it as much as your prospective customer. At this point, it's helpful to remind yourself again that you believe that the product or service you are selling will benefit this person and make her life or business better or more efficient.

Keep in mind as you're dialing the phone that the person (you) with the most information has the advantage. Before you push that first button, you must learn as much as you can about the other person's situation. Not only do you want to appear more knowledgeable but you'll want to be able to incorporate this information into your negotiation tactics. How do you do this? As I mentioned earlier, you do research on the Internet, at the library, and by reading his company materials.

When it comes time to talk for the first time, you'll want to ask a lot of questions. Remember, this isn't about you but about what you can offer and provide for this person. After introducing your product or service, there's nothing wrong with asking:

- "What time frame are you working with on this project?"
- "What do you see as the first priority in getting this installation put in place?"

At the same time you're learning about your customer's attitudes, hot buttons, and possible quirks, you also want to learn as much as you can about his other contacts—your competitors.

Asking something like "What other companies have you spoken to about this problem?" is not out of line. It will help you defend your price point and knock out the possibility your prospective customer will use the competition's price as a negotiating point.

Don't argue. Nothing says "No Deal" better than a strong defensive position from you. You must recognize that you're most probably going to get objections from your prospective customer. This is an accepted part of doing business. It's the back and forth of negotiating until you arrive at a point where you feel like each of you has gotten a good deal.

Don't take his objections personally and don't assume he's not interested. Expressing concerns and doubts shows interest. If he doesn't ask questions or challenge your sales points, as the popular bestselling book title says, he's just not that into you. As you provide answers, keep your style nonconfrontational and remember that your goal is to not just establish this one sale—but to begin a relationship that could last for many years to come.

Keep your answers short and to the point. Answer honestly but don't go overboard. By talking too much, it might appear that you're trying too hard to justify your product or service. This could send a caution sign to your customer. He might ask himself, "Why is she trying so hard to sell me on this? And that hesitation might just talk you right out of the sale.

If, after talking to your customer, it is obvious you cannot solve his problem and that your company's service or products are not the best match for each other in this particular deal, there's nothing wrong with suggesting someone at another company who can be of assistance.

By being helpful, you've shown you're a person whom your prospective customer can count on to provide truthful answers and solutions to meet his company's needs. A few weeks later, follow up with a handwritten note and a business card to express your concern—you want to know that his company's needs in this particular matter have been met. Chances are, he'll put your business card in his Rolodex and remember who you are the next time you call.

Negotiate with Confidence

Think of the last time you bought a new car or got bids to have your house painted. Did you enjoy the negotiating process? Most people, because they lack confidence and want to get along with others, hesitate to negotiate. Many look at asking for a price to be reduced or a discount to be given as bold, unattractive behavior.

Don't let it bother you when your customer, who is most assuredly comfortable dealing with sales representatives, objects to your offer when you prepare to close the sale. Expect her to appear a bit insulted or incredulous—better yet, if you've prepared your offer wisely, perhaps you'll be pleasantly surprised when she accepts the deal as is.

In order to feel confident in your negotiating skills, you should practice every chance you get. For example, ask for a price break when the shirt you want to buy at the department store is missing a button. When the salesman comes back with a price, tell him politely, "You'll have to do better than that." The worst that can happen—you'll buy another shirt at another store. Remember to treat others how you wish to be treated—be persistent but be pleasant and polite. And know when it's time to walk away.

After the First Sale

You've delivered the service, ordered the product, and initiated the billing. If you think you're finished, you're wrong—your work is only half done. If business is slow or you have a small number of customers you do business with, following up is relatively easy. It's when business is booming and orders are increasing that good customer service can slip.

Remember your customer is only your customer as he's placing this specific order with you. After that transaction, he can go anywhere, to anyone, for his next business deal. By ensuring good customer service, you increase your chances of return business and referrals by your customer to others. You send them away happy and they return with not only more of their business but possibly with more contacts for you.

Anyone with sales training can sell one time. But it is your follow-up that will determine whether or not your customer gives you a repeat business. The one true statement about customer service is that your customer will judge you by what you do, not what you say you'll do. Here are some simple things to keep in mind:

- *Be reliable.* If you tell your customer you'll have someone there to install the new computers you've sold him on Tuesday, and no one shows up until Thursday, you've lost credibility—and your customer. The same is true if you set an appointment and don't keep it. Nothing annoys more than a broken promise.

- *Continue to listen to your customer.* Perhaps you've solved one dilemma for your customer but now he has another. Pick up on this through continuing conversations. Again, ask questions. You might be able to solve this new problem or know of someone who can. Chances are, you'll come away with another sale. If not, you've at least increased your reliability and helpfulness.

- *Deal with disappointment.* You've sold your customer a specific part for the main machine in his factory. Problem is—what was delivered isn't working. If possible, get out of your office and into her place of business. See for yourself what needs to be done. Give this matter your utmost attention. Find out when the proper part can be delivered and follow up on the order until the correct part is put in place. There's nothing like hands-on, personalized customer service.

- *Go the extra mile.* During a phone conversation with your prospective customer he asks you if you know where he can buy the newest widget on the market. Though your company doesn't sell it, direct him to a resource that does. Though you might not get that sale, he's likely to remember you—especially when you call again to ask how that new widget is working.

Remember, everyone makes mistakes—it's what you do about them and how you learn from them that is important. Customers, whether new or old, appreciate honesty and the hard work you put in to making the situation right.

There may be times when you lose control of the sales interaction, you talk too much, or you don't do enough research. It happens to veteran sales pros as well as clammy-palmed new reps.

What your customer ultimately wants is that "something special" she can't get anywhere else. As Walt Disney once said, "Do what you do so well that people want to bring their friends to see you do it again." One trip to a Disney theme park in Florida or California will convince you, Mr. Disney knew what he was talking about. To a successful cold-call salesman or one who travels door-to-door, satisfying the customer so much that he returns again and again is the only thing that matters.

Getting Past the Assistant

Okay. But what happens when you cold call and, instead of getting the prospect on the phone, you get her assistant or the company receptionist? Use the "Answer/Ask" strategy.

The Answer/Ask, or "A/A" Strategy, was invented by sales trainer Bill Bishop. The technique basically involves "turning the tables" on secretaries, receptionists, and other filters by answering their questions with a question. As Bill explains[2]:

> My A/A Strategy is a technique guaranteed to get you past the secretary to the decision maker. The first A stands for "answer." This means you answer filters' questions, instead of playing evasive cat-and-mouse games that tell filters you are a salesperson.
>
> The second A stands for "ask," meaning you ask filters a question after answering theirs. This forces them to stop and answer your question, which in turn prevents them from asking additional filtering questions, and increases your chances of getting the decision maker on the line.
>
> For example:
> Receptionist: "Good morning. Acme Widgets."
> You: "Ms. Big, please."
> Receptionist: "May I tell her who's calling?"
> You: "Would you tell her you have Bill Bishop holding, please?"
> See the technique? If you simply answer "It's Bill Bishop calling," you set the secretary up for her next screening question, designed to block your call. But instead, when you answer with a question—"Would you tell him you have Bill Bishop holding, please?"—the reasonable

response is for the filter to answer in the affirmative and put you through.

Once in a while you'll get a tough filter who will come back with the second filtering question. Here's how the A/A Strategy handles it:

Receptionist: "And who are you with, Mr. Bishop?"

You: "Would you tell him my company is Bill Bishop Associates, please?"

Again, if you just said, "My company is Bill Bishop Associates," the likely response would be, "And what is this in reference to?" or "Does he know you?"

Will answer/ask eliminate all secretarial screening? No. But it will reduce the number of screening questions and get you through in a certain percentage of cases where you wouldn't normally have been connected.

Potential Problems with Cold Calling

Think about the last time a telemarketer interrupted you during your work-day or at home just as you sat down to have dinner with your family. Chances are you didn't eagerly rush to pick up the telephone and engage in a quality conversation that resulted in a business transaction.

More than likely, you let the call go to voice mail or you politely—or angrily—expressed your irritation at the intrusion or your disinterest in the sales pitch and abruptly ended the exchange. In the back of your mind you might have even given thanks you weren't the guy on the other end of the line attempting to make the cold call sale.

But what if you were?

Calling someone you don't know can conjure up a lot of fear. After all, you know almost nothing about the names typed on the paper in front of you. You know the telephone number, perhaps the address, and the chance they may be interested in whatever it is you're selling. The possibility of rejection is at least 50/50.

Your palms begin to sweat as you entertain the scenario of the person on the other end of the line yelling or insulting you—or worse—hanging up before you've gotten the first sentence out of your mouth. As you sit there with the receiver in one hand and the buzz of the dial tone echoing in your ear, it occurs to you—this is something you're going to have to do again . . . and again . . . and again.

To be successful at cold calling, and to enjoy what you do for a living, you've got to have a plan—and work it—or you won't last a week in the world of sales. Not only do you have to generate new business; you must continuously develop and nurture your business contacts and partnerships in order to keep revenue flowing in the future. How you view the act of cold calling will play an important part in how successful—and satisfied—you'll be with this aspect of your job.

Be Positive About a Negative

Yes, cold calling can have negative connotations. Hearing a stranger's stilted cheery greeting as he unexpectedly intrudes into private time can start things off on the wrong foot. Getting things moving in a positive direction starts with how you view your job as a sales professional.

"I believe in the products I sell," says John, a veteran sales representative. "I know how each tool works, what it's capable of, how it's used, cleaned, and stored. I know the history behind its development, how long it can be expected to last and, most importantly, what my customer needs and what the competition has to offer."

It's obvious from John's thorough knowledge of his product that he is confident about the calls he makes and the information he shares with his prospective customers. He's not just motivated to make a sale; he's genuinely excited to share his knowledge and personal experience with others who he believes would benefit from his product.

When you pick up the telephone to make your first call, how do you feel? Ask yourself the following questions:

- Are you enthusiastic about the product or service you're offering or are you irritated that this is just one more thing you have to do?
- Are you hesitant about the quality of what you're selling?

- Do you feel like you're bothering your prospective customer?
- Do you find yourself apologizing for taking up her time?

If you've answered yes to any of these questions, put down the phone and do your homework, because if you don't believe in what you're selling, how can you expect that someone else will?

When you're calling a person you don't know, your voice will reflect your apprehension and any bit of hesitation you may have. This immediately puts you in the one-down position and can hinder your ability to make the sale.

When you cold call a prospective customer, you are at a disadvantage because you cannot see his facial expressions or read his body language. In turn, your customer relies on your voice to transmit your personality.

Here are a couple things that will help:

- Buy a cheap hand mirror and stand it in a place where you can see and look at yourself as you make phone calls.
- Have a friend record you on videotape or record your voice on a tape recorder. Speak slowly, distinctly, and in a natural tone of voice.
- Smile as you talk. It will help your neck muscles relax and your voice will sound more natural and reflect a positive quality.
- As you play back your recording, try to observe and listen as a stranger would. Watch or listen to the recording several times to pick up on the subtle nuances.

Do you sound like a person you would like to do business with? Once you identify and acknowledge your shortcomings, you'll work very hard to correct them.

Gain Permission to Proceed

When cold calling, try asking prospects, "Am I catching you at a bad time right now?" This gives you several advantages on the call:

- Many prospects will say, "No, it's okay"—giving you, in essence, permission to proceed with the sales calls.

- With those who say they are busy, you can set a phone appointment for a call-back.

- When you make that call-back, and the secretary asks, "Is she expecting your call?", you can truthfully answer, "yes."

- You will stand out from the crowd by demonstrating to prospects you are respectful of their time.

If the prospect says, "No, this is a good time," she is giving you permission to proceed. If she says, "Yes, it's a bad time," ask when a good time is and call back then. It's that simple.

Get to Know Your Customer

Productive, positive relationships are built on trust and integrity. Verbal and nonverbal communication tells your customers a lot about you. They will be more apt to want to continue business dealings with you if you have a few things in common and you enjoy doing business together.

Consider any of the following:

- Take a class that interests you—perhaps even something that relates to your customer's business.

- Skim the front page of the newspaper in your customer's area so you'll be up on area news.

- Read that new bestseller everyone's talking about.

- Has your customer's company recently opened a branch office in a city you know nothing about? A trip to the local bookstore's travel shelf will help you learn more about the area.

Think of it this way—your customer is considering investing his time, energy, and financial resources in what you have to offer. He expects you to know not only about his business but his industry as well.

Become familiar with trends and problems in his field. Read his company's annual report, catalogs, and brochures as well as the trade publications for that particular business. Sign up to receive the company newsletter—

that way you'll stay abreast of internal changes such as restructuring of departments, new appointments, and recent hires.

Honing your social skills and developing the ability to carry on casual conversations that show an interest in the other person and knowledge about her surroundings will help you develop a harmonious relationship that works for both of you. Instead of coming off as obnoxious or aggressive, you can create an atmosphere in which it's pleasant to conduct business.

Face Your Fear

Cold calling brings with it the fear of the unknown. As the telephone rings, questions begin to race through your mind—what if this person's rude? What if she asks me a question I don't know the answer to? What if my mind goes blank? What if I get through and I can tell he's not interested? How do I end the call?

As with any other challenge, the best thing to do is dissect the fear one element at a time. If you're clear about the purpose of your call and you're knowledgeable about your product or service, you're halfway home. A bit of positive self-talk will take you the rest of the way.

Consider the following:

Self-Defeating Dialogue: He's probably got other things to do and I'm intruding.

Self-Empowering Dialogue: I've got a product that can help him cut his expenses by 40 percent and he needs to know about it.

Self-Defeating Dialogue: If I try to close this sale, she'll probably say no.

Self-Empowering Dialogue: This opportunity will lead to a win-win situation for both of us.

Self-Defeating Dialogue: After I explained everything, she still said no.

Self-Empowering Dialogue: She came up with an objection—that tells me she listened closely enough to what I had to say.

Your confidence will grow as you plan each step of your sales call. In the meantime, here are some ideas to help put things in a positive light:

- Buy an inexpensive corkboard and hang it close enough to your telephone so that you can see it while you're making your cold calls. On the board, hang clippings, thank-you notes, testimonials from satisfied customers, and other nice things you've received.
- Keep names and telephone numbers of close friends and colleagues nearby so that when you need a bit of emotional support, they're only one phone call away.
- Start a file of "fan mail"—letters, notes, and e-mails—from satisfied customers. Rereading these after a particularly hard "I'm not interested" reply will help you bounce back quickly.
- Visualize yourself walking out the door with a signed contract in hand and a promise for future business. Close your eyes and "feel" the emotions of achieving a win-win situation.

Get Organized

Here are a few tips that will come in handy as you prepare for your cold call session:

- Compile a list of happy customers to use for "name dropping" during your conversation. Using another company's name creates validation, increases prospect confidence, and adds credibility.
- Make a list of the most important points you want to share with your prospect rather than reading your script word-for-word.
- When making multiple calls, avoid confusion by printing your prospective customer's home page from her company's website and write your notes on it. As you continue to make calls, you'll have the advantage of having your notes on the appropriate page.
- Prepare a list of the most common questions or objections your customer is likely to have and the appropriate responses for each. Make sure each of your answers is complete and addresses the particular point he has raised. Always validate his concern.
- Though you've made notes and lists, never sound like you are reading from your computer screen or pad of paper. Not only does this sound

fake, it tells your customer you're not interested enough in what you're selling to be able to converse about it.

- When it comes time to set an appointment, ask for a specific time. Say something like, "Let's plan on Tuesday at 9:00 A.M.–will that work for you?" By doing so, you're taking the initiative to get the ball rolling.

The first impression you make lasts forever even it takes as little as sixty seconds to complete. For cold calling, some sales pros dress as if a face-to-face meeting has been planned.

"It makes me feel more in character and gives me that extra edge," says Tom Regan, a manufacturer's representative. "I also stand when I make my calls. I feel like I have a lot of energy and my voice sounds more natural."

Get Comfy

You'll do your best work if you're comfortable and relaxed. Keep a glass of water at hand and don't chew gum or eat while you're on the telephone. Make sure you have all the office supplies–pens, pencils, paper, stick-it notes–at hand. The last thing you want is to be scrambling around for a pen that doesn't skip or a clean eraser at the end of your pencil.

A few other suggestions:

- Sitting at a desk and talking on the phone for long periods of time can cause neck, back, and wrist strain. Keep your spine and head upright. Sit back in your chair and keep your feet flat on the floor. Hold your arms in a comfortable position.
- Every twenty minutes, stand up and stretch. Take a short walk to keep your circulation moving.
- Consider investing in a headset. It makes you more comfortable when you speak and leaves your hands free to take notes or type on your keyboard.

Be Yourself

Some people feel more comfortable and confident if they are surrounded by familiar things such as a favorite fountain pen or a finely made leather briefcase. While these items can represent success, the art of being yourself is the most important trait you can present to your new contact.

Here are a couple of commonsense strategies to keep in mind:

- When following up with a written note, use quality white or light-colored stationary. Consider investing in personalized notecards.
- Remember to include your business card with your correspondence.
- Return phone calls promptly. If you're late returning a prospective customer's phone call, don't think she isn't wondering how late her order will be in arriving.
- Be an attentive listener. If you find yourself leaning forward, nodding your head in agreement, or raising an eyebrow at a question, don't worry—this indicates you're actively listening.
- Speak your customer's language. Make sure you understand acronyms and the business lingo for the field in which your prospective customer is a pro.
- Pay attention to common courtesies such as using correct grammar, remembering to say thank you, and staying aware of the amount of time you're taking up in the conversation.
- Don't interrupt or monopolize the conversation and always make sure the other person has finished conveying the message before you speak.
- Ask questions. Though you're on the telephone, make sure you give your prospective customer your full attention. Don't try to be someone you're not, thinking it will get you in the door. Your goal is to develop a long-term, productive relationship with your prospective customer.

Keep in mind, you'll hopefully be talking to this person over and over so the relationship you're beginning to build must be an authentic one. Be friendly, yet business-like. When you clearly see the concerns and perspectives of your customer, you are better equipped to help him solve his problem and your credibility will be established.

Through the course of your sales career, you'll place thousands of phone calls. You'll get thousands of rejections and thousands of sales. Every call you make will be a learning experience.

Relax, have fun, and don't take every "no" so seriously. When you reduce cold calling down to its basic format, you've got a product or service you believe in so much you want to spread the word and have other people be as thrilled as you are about it.

Keep in mind, the purpose of your cold call is not to convince someone to purchase a service or goods they don't need or want. If that's your goal, you'll never succeed. Your efforts should instead be focused on finding those customers who have a need to fill or a problem to solve. You have the answer they are looking for. It all begins with dialing the phone and asking yourself the question—would you buy from you?

Notes

1. John Brentlinger, *The Little Blue Book of Selling* (Samurai Publishing, 2004).
2. Robert Bly, *Selling Yourself* (New York: Henry Holt, 1992).

How to Develop a Magnetic Telephone Voice and Manner

People hate telephone sales and telemarketers but, with the right tonality and content, you can warm up a sales call and actually attract people to you over the phone.

The telephone has a great deal of power, yet as a basic business instrument it is often misused. How many times have you been put off by a receptionist who gives you a grilling to rival that given Al Capone by the FBI? Or been greeted by an anonymous "hold, please" and left hanging in a silent void for what seems like an eternity? At best, these kinds of encounters are annoying. At worst, they can create a negative impression and sour a relationship.

The first contact many people have with you is over the phone. They probably will form a lasting impression of you on the basis of that conversation. Fortunately, with a little tact and attention to what you say and how you say it, you can use the phone as an effective tool in getting and keeping cooperation, sales, and goodwill.

Mind Your Manners

Promptness counts. Answer your calls on the first or second ring, if possible. This gives the caller the impression that you are responsive and efficient. Occasionally, you may have to delay answering a call to finish an urgent task or because you were momentarily away from your desk. But no office phone should ring more than four times before being picked up by someone. Otherwise, you may risk losing a valuable call.

When you answer, identify yourself. A "hello" is not sufficient; give your name and department. By saying "Mike Bugalowski, Sales," you give callers the information they need, and you also prompt them to identify themselves in return. This also shows that you are businesslike and ready to be of service.

Apply this rule even when picking up the phone for someone else. Say, "Todd Pitlow's office, Mike Bugalowski speaking," so callers will know someone is taking responsibility for helping them.

Answer and place your own calls. Screening calls via a receptionist or an assistant wastes time and annoys callers. If possible, answer your own phone. Callers will appreciate the fact that you're available for them and that they don't have to be put through the third degree to reach you. Similarly, placing your own calls circumvents the ego game of seeing which executive waits for the other.

If you must have your calls screened in order to work efficiently, have your secretary do so politely and briefly. Don't make callers feel as if they're being discriminated against. Instead of saying, "Who's calling?"—or worse, "Who is this?"—which challenges the caller, ask, "May I tell him who is calling, please?"

If you are available to speak to only certain people, ask your secretary to first say that you're in a meeting and then ask, "May I tell her who called?" If the caller is someone you want to talk to, your assistant can then say, "Here he is now," or, "Let me see if I can get her for you."

Offer an explanation as to why someone is unavailable. Better to say, "He's in a meeting right now," "She's on another line," or "He's out of the office," than simply "He's unavailable" or "She can't come to the phone."

By giving more information to callers, you come across as being honest and up front, so they are less likely to feel they are being lied to or discriminated against.

Always offer to help the caller yourself, or find someone who can, or take a message and personally see that it gets to the right person. Don't ask the person to call back later; this is inconsiderate of the caller's time and money.

When screening calls, avoid using phrases that seem to challenge callers or imply that they may not be worth talking to. For example, the screening phrase, "Does he know you?" is offensive because it puts callers in the embarrassing position of having to guess whether you remember them, and it implies that any caller not known will not be able to get through to you.

Some other screening phrases to avoid (along with our reactions to them):

"Will she know where you're from?" (I don't know; I'm not a mind reader.)

"And what is this in reference to?" (Do you want the long version or the short version?)

"What company are you with?" (Does he talk only with people from companies? Too bad, I'm with the IRS.)

"And you're from . . . ?" (Kentucky, originally.)

"And what does this concern?" (His wife's gambling debt.)

People don't like to get the runaround. So if you need to transfer someone, first explain why and where you are switching the call. It's also wise to give the caller the extension or number, in case the call gets disconnected.

Cover yourself. Leaving a phone unattended is a surefire way to lose important calls and irritate those trying to reach you. We've all had the frustrating experience of calling a business and letting the phone ring ten or fifteen times with no answer. When that happens, we get angry and think, "What a poorly run company they must be to let the phone ring so long."

If there is no one available in your office to answer your calls while you are away, have the calls transferred to a receptionist or someone else who agrees to cover for you.

Be sure to tell that person where you are going, when you will be back, and any telephone number where you can be reached. Then collect your messages and return your calls promptly.

When you take a message, listen carefully and write down everything. Get the person's name, telephone number, affiliation, and the name of the person or department the caller is trying to reach. Even when callers are in a rush, don't be afraid to ask them to repeat spellings, pronunciations, and numbers if you didn't hear clearly the first time. Taking complete, accurate messages avoids confusion, and ensures that calls can be returned promptly.

No one likes to be put on hold. But if it's necessary, first explain why you need to leave the line, how long you'll be gone, and then ask if the caller can hold. Wait for a reply; no one likes being put on hold before they have a chance to object. But when you ask, you'll find that most people say "OK" and appreciate your courtesy. When you return to the phone, thank the caller by name for waiting.

Make sure the caller isn't on hold for more than two minutes. If you need to be away from the phone longer than that, ask if the caller would prefer that you call back. Promise to call back at a specific time, and do so.

Everyone has a bad day now and then, but it's not smart to show it in person or on the phone. Anger, impatience, or simple boredom can come through a phone line quite clearly and make a caller defensive or nervous. If you are unpleasant or brusque on the phone, people may go out of their way to avoid dealing with you.

So, no matter what your mood, strive to be pleasant and alert throughout a conversation. When people call at a bad time, ask if you can get back to them again. Mention a specific time when you will call them back.

A good rule to remember is to treat callers the way you would guests in your office or home. You'll win their respect and goodwill. Courtesy and attentiveness can only help you and your company in improved public image, better customer relationships, and increased sales.

Use Your Telephone Wisely

Have you ever noticed during a phone conversation how many people say, "I think" or "I feel?" Do they interject "hmm" or "uh" or "you know?"

often into their sales delivery? Are there uncomfortable lulls in the conversation? When those things occur, you get the distinct impression that the person on the other end of the line is not demonstrating a commanding presence. A decision maker will not have as much confidence in a person who doesn't use phrases like "I can," "I will," or "I know."

Learn to speak in your customers' language. Learn the acronyms for their policies and procedures. Avoid using any terminology they may not understand or recognize. With today's technology, it is easy to forget not everyone is as familiar with techno-speak and specialized jargon as perhaps you are. Avoid getting frustrated and making your prospective customer feel inadequate. The last thing you want is for her to keep asking you for an explanation.

PROSPECT REPELLANT #6:

Not getting the prospect's name right.

People have a strong negative reaction when you mispronounce their name, get the name wrong, or misspell it.

So be sure to get the prospect's name right. When a prospect gives you their name, say it over and over in your head to remember it.

You might want to use a memory trick to recall the name. For instance, if the prospect's name is Susan Cohen, you might think, "She is going to sue a cone." Or if he is Kenny Baker, think "Can he bake her?"

If the name is difficult to understand, ask the prospect to repeat it. Then you say it back to her, and ask if you got it right. Also get the prospect's card to have the name in writing.

Ask prospects how they want to be addressed. An older prospect might resent a young salesperson calling him by his first name, and prefer to be addressed as Mr. Some people are sensitive about their nicknames or initials; John D. Smith might want to be called "JD," and Jeffrey Jones might dislike being called "Jeff."

For business prospects, build a personal relationship with the prospect's assistant or secretary. In my business, when an assistant helps us in some way, we send a nice box of gift chocolates with a personalized thank-you note. From the enthusiastic thank-you e-mails I get, I am convinced this is both rare and appreciated.

Often, assistants control the prospect's schedule and activities, as well as what correspondence and phone calls get through. When the assistant is your ally, your sales job becomes much easier.

How you use the telephone says a great deal about you and your business. In the world of cold call sales, that first connection is also your first contact with your prospective customer and the all-important first impression he receives is made. The following phone tips will help you cold call with confidence and develop valuable on-going business relationships:

- When you are expecting a customer's call, always answer before the third ring. This shows her that you're attentive to your business and ready to take the call.

- Use a warm, enthusiastic—but natural—tone of voice. Smiling helps. (Hint: This also works when you are recording or leaving a voice message.)

- When you're calling a new customer, always identify yourself and your organization right up front. Make sure you enunciate clearly. Speak slowly but naturally and in an audible but not shouting tone. If you're hesitant about the proper pronunciation of a name, ask the receptionist before you're connected just to be on the safe side.

- Don't use slang or a conversational, intimate tone with someone who is still a stranger to you. Remember—you want to put your best self forward and create that all-important positive first impression. Answer with "certainly" instead of "not a problem." Train yourself to speak professionally by talking into a recorder and playing it back to hear exactly how you sound. You may be surprised at how many "you know's" sneak into your dialogue.

- If you've promised to get information back to your caller, make sure you do so within one business day. Any longer and your customer will assume he's pretty far down on your priority list and he'll add your name to the bottom of his list as well—or worse—throw your contact information into the garbage can.

- If your phone call is interrupted, politely ask your customer if you can call him back. There's nothing that will make a customer feel more ill at ease than to be in the middle of explaining his company's problem (which you can help solve!) and you say in a distracted voice, "Can you hold on a sec?" You might as well say good-bye right then and there.

- If a call-waiting beep comes through, let it go. No one is more important than the person you've got on the line.

- A lot of people feel very self-conscious when they're put on a speakerphone. Unless it's understood that others will be listening in, do not put the person on a speakerphone without asking his permission. Doing so without his knowledge sends a clear message that you are not being attentive or considerate.

- When you leave your office, use an answering machine to get the calls when you can't. Again, speak clearly, enunciate correctly, and give the necessary information in a friendly voice. Make sure you keep your message up to date. It's not a good thing when a customer calls on December 1 and your voice message says you'll be out of the office until the day after Thanksgiving.

- If you're working from home, install a separate work line in a private office. There's nothing that says "unprofessional" more than a ringing doorbell and a barking dog or a small child who answers the phone. And speaking of phone installation, investigate the bundled packages of services your local carrier offers. In this age of technology, you should take advantage of call forwarding, call waiting, and the other services offered.

- Do not answer your cell phone in public places. Though conducting business is important, it is no one else's business nor are they interested in what you have to say as you chatter away in a restaurant, movie theater, or other public place. If you answer your cell phone during a lunch meeting with a prospective customer, you might as well say to her, "Excuse me, but someone more important than you is calling and I have to talk to them now." Instead, consider putting your phone on vibrate, and at the appropriate time, excuse yourself from your guest to check the message. If you must reply, send a short text message notifying your caller when you'll be returning to the office.

More Telephone Techniques

Have you ever had to hold the receiver about a foot away from your ear to dim the voice on the other end? Or, conversely, have you ever strained to make out what the person on the other end was saying? Then you know how important a good speaking voice is in effective telephone communications.

When you make a call, put the receiver against your ear. Hold the mouthpiece close to your lips, and speak clearly in a normal tone of voice. If people can't understand you because you talk too fast, make a conscious effort to slow down. These tips may seem elementary, but they can help prevent garbled communications and listener frustration.

Brief conversations save time, and your listener will be grateful for them. Everyone enjoys a certain degree of personal conversation—such as "How are you?" or "How was your trip?"—but lengthy personal discourses or general ramblings on are inappropriate, and probably boring to most people.

It's a good idea, therefore, to stick to the point and to be prepared when you are planning or expecting a call. Write down the major points you want to cover on a sheet of paper; when you talk, look at the sheet and check off each point as it is discussed. This technique will help you keep on the subject and avoid getting sidetracked. If an unexpected subject comes up, and you need to get more information, explain this to the caller and make arrangements to call back with the answers.

Be gracious and pleasant when ending a call even if you're not happy with the outcome. Thank the person for his time. Summarize points agreed on or actions to be taken. Say "good-bye" so he will know you are finished.

In fact, it's best to let him hang up first, so that you don't cut him off inadvertently. And when you hang up, do it gently. A slammed receiver creates jangled nerves and a negative impression.

Following these simple tips will put you ahead of the crowd in dealing with colleagues, superiors, suppliers, and customers. True, you may find yourself handling more calls because people like dealing with you, but this brings with it increased opportunities for success. By mastering the fine art of telephone conversation, you will enhance your reputation as well as your company's.

Starting Your Day on the Telephone

Begin your day of cold calling by putting yourself in the best frame of mind possible. Kate, who changed careers at the age of forty-five, now works as an agent for a large Midwest realty firm. Without an established customer base, she must rely on cold calls to grow her business. "I get up early and take time to get ready for my day," she says.

Her morning routine begins with a half hour of stretching exercises and aerobics followed by a well-balanced breakfast and another fifteen minutes either reading something motivational or just being quiet. It is this time that Kate uses to get spiritually and emotionally centered for the day.

"My exercise program builds my endurance and flexibility," she says, "but more importantly, it gives me the energy I need to keep pace with my customers." Her fifteen minutes of quiet helps remove any discord or irritation that might be starting to build: "Just that little bit of time helps put me in a more positive frame of mind. By the time I walk out the door, I'm ready to be the most eager, helpful real estate agent on the planet."

Creating Online Presentations for Telephone Selling

How much extra money could you make by closing just one or two additional sales a day? Using modern technology, you can now increase the effectiveness of your telephone presentations by adding visuals your prospect can see over the Web.

According to marketing expert Roger C. Parker, you can increase the effectiveness of your telephone call by up to 400 percent when your customers and prospects can see, as well as hear, what you're talking about. He says that customers and prospects are visually oriented: They process and retain 75 percent of the information they see, compared to about 15 percent of the information they hear.

"When you invite a customer or prospect to view an online presentation while talking to you on the phone, your ability to close the sale immediately skyrockets," notes Roger. Following are his six steps for creating your first online presentation.[1]

Step 1: *Desired Result.* Start by identifying what you want to accomplish during each phone call. Ask yourself questions like:

- What is the primary message I want to communicate?
- What action do I want my customer or prospect to take?
- What information can I provide to convince them to take the desired action?

Your answers to these questions will determine the key points to emphasize in your upcoming calls.

Step 2: *Benefits.* Next, list the benefits customers and prospects will enjoy after they buy your product or service. Translate every feature into a specific and measurable benefit, organized in terms of importance.

Step 3: *Framework.* Open your presentation program and create an "empty" set of visuals with just titles. This creates a framework for developing your online presentation. Do not complete each visual! Simply create an empty presentation visual, with a benefit-oriented title, for every point you want to make during your upcoming call. (You'll finish each visual later.)

HINT: Save your framework as a template to save time creating future presentations for additional products and services.

Step 4: *Provide Proof.* Next, go through your visuals one-by-one—and complete each one by adding the necessary text and graphics. Communicate benefits as specifically and visually as possible. Translate products or services into added revenue dollars or specific time and money savings.

Show rather than tell. Translate words into information graphics, like tables, charts, and graphs, to visually communicate:

- *Comparisons*: Before and after revenue increases or cost reductions.
- *Trends:* Economic or competitive pressures that add details and urgency to your recommendations.
- *Time and Sequence:* Show what you're going to do, who's going to do it, and when.

Add photographs to personalize and reinforce case studies and testimonials. Use logos, rather than words, to emphasize case studies and satisfied customers.

Step 5: *Contingency Visuals*. Next, anticipate objections that prospects may bring up during your call. List as many potential objections as possible and decide how you will respond to each one. Translate your responses into additional visuals that you will only show if the prospect brings up specific objectives. The most common objectives involve price, competitive advantages, ease of use, and your firm's experience.

Step 6: *Upload and Rehearse*. Review, then use your program's "Save as" command to convert visuals to the appropriate format for online display. Upload your presentation to the server where you can control what your prospects see on the screen of their computer as you talk. Add filenames that describe each visual's contents to you.

Rehearse your presentation until you are comfortable going from point to point, and accessing the contingency visuals. View your Web-based presentation as a "work in progress." You can update it by preparing additional visuals as new objectives come up. And consider creating personalized visuals for specific customers, prospects, or products and services.

NOTE: You can find companies that can arrange teleconferences, Webinars, and other Web-based telephone presentations on the Vendors page of my website, www.bly.com.

Note

1. Roger C. Parker, *Guerilla Marketing and Design,* Vol. 4, #6. www.one pagenewsletters.com.

The Principle of Right Timing

When you approach the prospect at the right time, whether it's to ask for an appointment or close the sale, the response will be positive. When you approach at the wrong time, you'll instantly repel him or her and derail the sale. I call this the Principle of Right Timing. This chapter shows how to (a) know when it's time to move the prospect to the next step in the buying cycle and (b) do this effectively, diplomatically, and without pressure.

ATTRACTION PRINCIPLE #7:

Prospects make decisions according to their own schedule, not yours.

> Buyers move according to their own timetable, not yours. Work within and respect their schedule, and they will want to do business with you. Try to push them to act before they're ready, and they'll resent the pressure . . . and want to avoid dealing with you. I call this the principle of Right Timing: Buyers won't buy before they are

ready. So your closing rate will increase dramatically if you adjust your selling efforts to their buying timetable.

Buyers do not like to be rushed into a decision, because they perceive that when they are not given time to think things through, they are more likely to make an error in their purchasing decisions. Experience shows this to be true. For instance, after 9/11, the federal government rushed to install security equipment, spending $4.5 billion. Now they are spending billions to replace much of that equipment, which doesn't work properly.

Magnetically unattractive salespeople view their role as selling as much as they can to as many people as they can as fast as they can, regardless of what is in the best interest of these prospects. Sales coach Tom Stoyan, who has a more magnetically attractive approach, defines selling as "helping people make buying decisions." And when you help people, you do it according to their schedule, not yours.

Smart marketing organizations instinctively know this and attempt to assess the prospect's degree of readiness as early in the sales cycle as possible. An example is a postcard that asks you to check off a box indicating when you are planning to buy a product, e.g., "immediately . . . in six months . . . next year . . . no immediate plans."

Prospects are rarely ready to buy when you call on them. So how do you make sure you call them when they are ready? To ensure that you'll be at the top of the prospect's vendor short list when it's time to make a decision, ask: "When do you think you'll be ready to go ahead with this?" Then call them at least two weeks before that date—to make sure you get in on time.

You can't make a sale until your prospect is ready to buy. In the book *Celebrate Selling*, sales trainer Aldonna Ambler identifies the four stages of prospect readiness:

- *Preoccupied.* Your prospects are so preoccupied with their current priorities they will not be responsive to your sales and marketing efforts.

- *Not Yet.* This group of prospects might be interested in what you have to offer, but need more time to complete their current priorities before taking on anything new.

- *Considering.* These prospects are considering adding the evaluation of your product or service to their next group of priorities.

- *Ready.* These prospects recognize your topic as a high priority and are ready to discuss details. Unless you can get the opportunity to make a presentation at this stage, your chances of getting the sale are extremely slim.[1]

Traditional sales training teaches you that (a) everyone is a potential buyer, and (b) you should try to close everyone right now.

Magnetic selling says that not everyone is a prospect, so your first job is to determine (a) who is a legitimate potential buyer of your service, and (b) in which of the four stages of readiness they are.

According to consultant Sean Woodruff:

We all love to shop. We all hate to be sold. The amateur salesperson doesn't understand this simple rule. Professional salespeople know the difference. Professionals build a rapport with the prospect by asking questions, listening, and presenting beneficial solutions that answer the questions. While a professional is selling, the prospect is buying or shopping. The two mesh together when the prospect trusts the pro.

Timing Is Everything

How many times have you been too early or too late with an idea? I've heard complaints from many who have failed because their timing just wasn't right.

Timing certainly has a lot to do with fads. You want to be involved at the beginning of a fad and not enter in the middle or at the end. But there are products that have just been introduced too early or too late, and that relates to timing too.

When do you introduce a new product? The answer really is quite simple: Nobody knows. "That's why every product I sell, I always test first," says mail-order entrepreneur Joseph Sugarman:

The consumer will always tell me if I'm too early or too late or right on target. When crime increased, it was good common sense to offer burglar alarms. It's just as important to know when timing is bad. We came out with a product called the Bone Fone, a portable radio worn around the neck. It was perfect timing until a product called the Walkman came out and killed our new product. Timing can kill a product or make it.

"No matter how well constructed your script is and no matter how professional you come across on the telephone, if your timing is off, none of the previous will mean a thing," writes Danielle Kennedy in *Double Your Income in Real Estate Sales*.

Kennedy says the best time of day to call prospects varies with audience, as follows:

Contractors	Before 9 A.M. and after 5 P.M.
Dentists	Before 9:30 A.M.
Doctors	9 to 11 A.M., 1 to 3 P.M., and 7 to 9 P.M.
Engineers	4 to 5 P.M.
Lawyers	11 A.M. to 2 P.M.
Executives	After 10:30 A.M.[2]

Learn the timing for the industries you sell to. Says sales trainer Art Siegel:

At one time, I sold printing to restaurants. At first, I cold called them as if they were any other business, but only for about two days. I quickly found out that most restaurant owners and managers don't want to talk to anyone but their customers during meal times, from 11:00 A.M. until 2:00 and from 5:00 until closing. Most restaurant owners do their buying during the morning lull in diners, and then do a little more intermixed with other administrative activities during the mid-afternoon. The pattern is not too different for most retailers, who have the most week-

day activity in their stores from mid-morning on, usually with a dip in the late afternoon.

On the other hand, automotive service establishments are flat-out busy first thing in the morning when people drop off their cars and late in the day when they pick them up, with another spike in activity around lunch time.

For many types of businesses, there is a natural cycle to the day that defines when they are most busy serving their customers. Your cold calls, whether by phone or in person, will be much more successful if you identify the peak and slack periods of the day for the businesses you call on, and call only during the slower times.

Most business people go through a consistent weekly cycle. First thing Monday morning they go to work on their to-do list with great aspirations of accomplishing more this week than they did last week. Supporting this pattern, more companies have their weekly staff meetings on Monday morning than any other time of the week. If you call on Monday morning, you are least likely to find the person you are calling available, and even less likely to find prospects who are willing to talk.

Friday afternoon is also usually a bad time: Most people are scrambling to wrap up as many items as possible on their list so they get home or to their favorite watering hole without delay. Call at this time, and you're almost certain to get a "Call me next week."

On the other days, mornings are usually a little better than afternoons. Just as the week starts with planning to get things done, and ends with a feverish effort to wrap things up, the typical work day starts with more of a planning structure, and then accelerates to intense work on projects. Your cold call fits in better with planning for the future than it does with interrupting concentration on completing a project.

The best and most successful times for cold calling are Monday, Tuesday, and Wednesday mornings, particularly Tuesday. At these times, people are as receptive to sales calls as they are likely ever to be.

Many companies measure their results on a monthly basis. They may be willing to talk with sales people early in the month, and then go into a mad scramble to achieve their monthly goals or complete their reports during the last week.

At other companies, people are equally accessible throughout the month, except on the first working day or the first Monday, when they hold their all-day monthly planning session. Still others may send all the executives away for off-site planning every quarter. Whenever possible, try to find out your prospect company's internal schedule to avoid those times when people you want to call on will not be available.

Scan local newspapers and business periodicals for names in the news—promotions, company events that might suggest opportunities, or just names of decision makers you don't already know about. When someone's name appears in the news, put them in your cold calling database, but don't contact them right away unless the news item reveals a problem in their company for which you offer a solution. Wait a month or more after someone's name appears in the news before you call.

Call during odd hours. Almost all decision makers work longer hours than their secretaries. If you want to increase the odds of your prospect answering the phone directly, without the clerical screen, try calling before 9:00, after 5:00, or during lunch time.

Also try Saturdays and legal holidays. Even if your prospect is not around then, you're more likely to get the prospect's voice mail box, where you can leave a personal message, rather than relying on a secretary to take down your message and pass it along.

When you are using a prospecting list or directory, work the list in reverse alphabetical order, from the back to the front. Reason: Your competitors are doing the opposite. That means that people who are at the end of lists tend to receive fewer sales contacts than those who are at the front, and when a new list comes out, people at the end are contacted later. You can give yourself an edge by always starting your cold calling from the end of the list, or picking an arbitrary point in the middle.

Whenever you attempt a cold call and are told: "I'm sorry, but he is in a meeting," ask: "What is generally the best time to reach him?" The person you speak with will usually give you a day of the week and a time of day when the prospect has more time to receive calls from salespeople. When you get through to a prospect, ask the best time to call him or her in the future.

ATTRACTION PRINCIPLE #8:

Timing is everything.

How frequently should you contact prospects? Neglect follow-up, and the prospect you don't keep in contact with may buy from someone else. Call too frequently, and you risk crossing the border from salesperson to pest.

So . . . how often should you follow up? There's no set formula, only some guidelines. A good starting point is the "Rule of Seven," formulated by marketing expert Dr. Jeffrey Lant. It states that to penetrate the buyer's consciousness and make significant penetration in a given market, you have to contact those people a minimum of seven times within an 18-month period.

This is slightly more than once every quarter. Although your frequency may be less or more, seven contacts within eighteen months—or four to five contacts within a year—is a good starting point for a follow-up plan.

You can modify this plan to suit your preferences. It's really up to you. Do what works. Don't get locked into a formula. If you get better results contacting hot prospects monthly, do so . . . as long as you keep below a frequency they will find annoying or offensive.

How do you know if you are following up too frequently? If just one or two prospects complain or seem annoyed, modify your schedule to accommodate them. But if 5 percent or more respond negatively to your frequency of follow-up, scale back on follow-up for that entire group of prospects. Use prospects' feedback to guide you in your efforts.

The rise of the Internet has given us a quantitative tool to determine precisely how frequent and persistent follow-up can be. In e-mail marketing, a key question is "How often can I e-mail my prospects without them becoming annoyed?"

The answer is simple: You look for a spike in the "opt-out rate"—the number of people who ask to be taken off your list whenever you send an e-mail marketing message or issue of your online newsletter.

The law requires that you include in every e-mail marketing message a mechanism for "opting out," meaning they can remove themselves from your e-list. You will have a few opt-outs every time you send an e-mail promotion to your list. But let's say you send an extra e-mail message this month and you suddenly get a lot more people opting out. That means your list is telling you that the frequency is too great and you should cut back.

We cannot measure "opt out" as precisely for sales follow-ups, but there are signs, nonetheless. For instance, if you are calling a prospect every week to ask about a proposal, and you can sense her getting annoyed, you know you have to follow up less persistently.

The best solution is to ask, "When should I get back to you about this?" Then call when she tells you, and not before.

What is the best time of day and the best days of the week to make follow-up calls? Opinions differ. For business prospects, Tuesday, Wednesday, and Thursday are the best follow-up days. On Mondays, people are too cranky; and on Fridays, they are too eager to get to the weekend. Mornings are usually better than afternoons, because most people have more energy in the morning.

Another principle of "right timing" is that you can, at times, make a sale simply because you catch someone at the right time. For business-to-business selling, I like to call prospects either early in the morning (before 9:00 A.M.), during lunch, or after 5:00 P.M.

Why? Because they are more likely to answer their phone at these times. During normal business hours, they are too busy, and let either an assistant or voice mail take the call.

Notes

1. Aldonna Ambler, *Celebrate Selling the Consultative Relationship Way* (Corte Madera, Calif.: Select Press, 1998).
2. Danielle Kennedy, *Double Your Income in Real Estate Sales* (New York: John Wiley & Sons, 1993).
3. Art Siegel, personal communication.

Magnetic Prospecting

From insurance agents to financial planners—almost all salesmen have re-lied on "cold calling" defined as "making uninvited calls or visits to a pro-spective customer with the intention of securing an interview leading to the placing of an order." It is a prospecting technique that's been around for a very long time and is still a popular way of creating new business for many companies.

Do a Google search for information on cold-calling sales techniques and you'll get 2,680,000 results in just a couple seconds. But how do you determine which prospecting methods will work for you—or better yet—which ones should you avoid so that your efforts don't end up angering a prospective customer?

Many managers of small businesses and large companies ask their sales force to spend time cold calling instead of having them meet face-to-face with individuals who want and need the products and services they are ready to buy. And yet many reps dread the experience. Perhaps you're one of them.

Prospecting for leads doesn't have to cause you to bite your fingernails to the quick. It can be a positive, motivating, and extremely profitable way to do business. However, if you haven't done your homework or prepared thoroughly in advance for your call or visit, all cold calling may get you is a lot of disappointment, a waste of valuable time, and lost sales.

Prospecting Lists and Directories

There are more potential customers for you than you have time to contact. How do you decide who you will contact? How do you decide who is a "qualified sale prospect"? If you're not working from an already established lead list, you can save yourself time and money if you think things through before picking up the telephone.

Begin by putting together an up-to-date list of contact names and phone numbers. There's nothing more frustrating and time wasting than wrong numbers and disconnected phone lines. Before you contact a list broker or the Standard Rate and Data Service (SRDS), you should establish as detailed a profile as you can of your ideal customer. By doing so, you'll stand a better chance of getting the kind of customer you really want—and who wants your products or services.

Next, set a list of criteria that the customers must meet in order for the sale to be mutually satisfying for both sides. Have a system in place that allows you to measure how well they fit into your sales plan.

You can purchase prospecting lists from brokers, private companies, or even the local chamber of commerce. You can attempt to create your own through trade associations, directories, and library research. If you are using a free list, make sure to have it professionally cleaned up to cut down on wrong and out-of-date information. Of course, one of the most valuable lists will be the one that contains the referrals you've obtained from current customers.

"Identify as many common characteristics of their best current customers as possible, then try to find more customers just like them," advises Vince Gupta in an article in *DM News* (May 2004). Business-to-business companies, for example, can develop a customer profile that includes data such as the number of employees; sales volume; geographic location; whether it is an independent company or a subsidiary, branch, or franchise; the title of the person making purchasing decisions; the industry sector and competitors; and use of technology.

If customer targets are consumers, salespeople can structure profiles around data such as their age, income bracket, and geographic region. Are they homeowners? If so, what is the value of their home? How long have they lived there? Do they have children? Pets? What are their hobbies or recreational interests? Do they order products over the Internet or through mail order?

The Prospecting Plan

As with everything else in life, proper preparation has its rewards. In your case, it can result in more positive experiences and higher sales. "Don't be impatient," says Bill Miller, a seventeen-year sales veteran and president of his own company that sells perishable tools and capital equipment for gear production. "Plan multiple calls and make the first call short just to introduce yourself." Miller adds, "It's also a good idea to make a connection with prospective customers by mentioning how it is you decided to call them. Give a reference name they know."

By having a prospecting plan in place, your chances are better that you'll get the kind of customer you want. An uncluttered, neatly organized desk and a prepared prospecting script will go a long way toward increasing your self-confidence and making the matter of cold calling a much more pleasant and productive experience.

Keep your contact list close by so that you'll always have easy access to it as you make call after call. Once the conversation has ended with a prospective customer, you should have a contact management system in place so you'll be able to keep track of your calls, what activity occurred, your next steps, and the date and time to follow up.

Do Your Homework

Most of us will agree that getting to know a stranger is hard to do—trying to sell a stranger a new product or service is nearly impossible unless you establish good rapport and a trusting relationship. The more you know about your prospect and his business before you make the call, the better your chances will be of setting up an appointment.

"One of the worst things to say to me as a prospective customer is 'What are your needs?'" says Ronald Fielding, group vice president of Hormel Foods Corporation, a Fortune 100 company with $5 billion in annual sales. "A good sales person already knows."

PROSPECT REPELLANT #7:

Not doing your homework.

Asking questions makes you magnetically attractive to prospects, since people like talking about themselves. They also like talking with people who are interested in them.

But prospects resent it when you ask them questions that you should already know. Say you are calling on Heinz. Asking them "What's your main product?" wastes their time. It's something you should already know: They make ketchup.

With the Internet, researching a business prospect is easier than ever. And prospects expect salespeople to have done their homework, and not waste their time asking them things they should already know before beginning their presentation or meeting.

Early in my career as a freelance copywriter, I called on an ad agency, hoping they would hire me to write ads for them. When I asked the agency owner "Who are your customers?" he pointed with disdain at a book on his shelf, turned away from me, and started working. The interview was over.

I thought he was rude. But the book he was pointing to, known as the "Red Book," listed all ad agencies, including his, and the major accounts they handled. So he was rude. But he was also right: I should have looked up his agency and learned what accounts they handled before coming to the meeting.

He taught me a valuable lesson, and I never repeated the mistake. As a salesperson, you will make mistakes throughout your entire career. You can't avoid it. What you can avoid is making the same mistake twice. Mistakes are not wasted experiences, as long as you learn from them.

According to Ron Fielding, when a salesperson contacts him, he looks for solid thinking and follow-through on important opportunities. Trust and reliability are the two most important things he must have in any business relationship.

Yet over the years Ron has been on the receiving end of several sales approaches that have not worked. He gives several examples and his responses[1]:

"Hello Ronald, I understand that you're managing Hormel International. I'd like to take you to lunch." Ron immediately knows this is a person who hasn't done his homework, because his position within the company changed five years ago. And why would he want to go to lunch with a complete stranger?

"Can you give me direction on how to do more business with your company?" Ron's response would be, "I don't have time to help you get connected."

"What are your needs?" Says Ron: "Why doesn't he already know before the call is made?"

The lesson? Even though you may be polite, pleasant, and persistent, if you talk and do not ask questions, or if you don't do your homework, you will most likely fail in your attempts to obtain a long-lasting customer.

Information gathering may take some time and effort but it pays off in the increased knowledge you'll gain about your prospective customer and the confident approach you'll present when you sit down to discuss how your product or service will help resolve problems within your targeted company and, of course, lead to higher revenue.

You can find out a lot about a company and its decision makers by researching the Internet and reading business journals, daily newspapers, and company literature. "Our sales associates are encouraged to research a company they are going to 'cold call,' so they know something about the company's business and their human resources needs," says a vice president of sales and marketing for a Charleston, North Carolina–based company.

Online subscription services, such as www.Hoovers.com, contain an extensive library of company information. Queries through your local newspaper's website or other places like the *New York Times* business section and the *Wall Street Journal* will yield a plethora of articles and stock news.

Don't neglect the obvious—check out the company's annual reports and their website for names of executive officers, revenue information, and any late-breaking company news. Remember: The more you know about your prospect before placing a cold call, the better your chance will be of getting a face-to-face appointment.

Find the Decision Maker

In today's busy environment, the men and women who have the power to make sales purchasing decisions can be hard to reach. Executive assistants screen calls and take messages that may not ever be returned.

Worst of all, if you aren't sure who to ask for and follow an automated voice system, you may find yourself caught in a never-ending message connection loop where the only "voice" you hear will be an artificial one. Your goal at this stage should be three-fold: locate your decision maker, determine through conversation if the need you have in mind can be filled with your product or service within the company, and then prepare your solution based on the information you've gathered.

Working your way through the maze of a company's organizational system can be difficult and time consuming. You don't want to get sidetracked into conversation only to find out the person on the other end of the line doesn't have the authority to purchase anything. Begin with the receptionist who answers the telephone.

The goal of your initial prospecting call is to discover the "who," the person responsible for making decisions to buy the solution you are offering. Keep in mind, at this stage of the game, you're not selling—you're gathering information.

Taking the time to find out additional facts will help diminish any nervousness about rejection and help you to build your confidence. Most people are willing to answer questions asked of them. They're also less defensive and more helpful when they don't feel like they're being set up for a sales pitch. If the receptionist says she is going to connect you with Mr. Smith's executive assistant, be sure you ask for the correct spelling and pronunciation before your call is transferred.

Another tactic you may want to try is to call the company headquarters and ask, depending on the size of the company, whether you can speak to the CEO or department vice president. Once again make sure you get the correct pronunciation and spelling.

Unless the business is small, you'll most probably be connected to the CEO's or vice president's assistant. The advantage in speaking to this person is that she deals on a day-to-day basis with higher level managers, and will most likely take your call. Cold calling can go much easier if you start at the top of the organization and work your way down. As in fishing, it's much easier to move downstream than it is to fight your way up.

If you don't already know the name of your contact, be honest and get to the point. You might say something like, "I hope you can help me. I'd like to speak to the person who takes care of purchasing (your product or service)," or "Could you connect me with the person who handles your building's outdoor landscaping?"

At this point, you might also want to consider asking a few more questions—after getting the name, of course. Remember to be gracious and thank her for the contact's name before adding, "So I don't take up too much of his time, there's probably some information you can help me with first."

Use exploratory questions that can't be answered by a simple "yes" or "no" and sharpen your listening skills to gather the information you need. Be clear about what is the purpose of your call. If it helps you to write a "script," by all means do so.

Some people prefer to write a script in longhand while others type it onto their computer screen along with questions that will further lead them through the cold call. Remember, you're not reading word-for-word, just using a couple of key words and statements to make your point. At all times, it is important to maintain a conversational tone of voice. The last thing anyone wants to hear is (and you've heard it a million times from the marketers who call you during dinner) a pre-scripted message the caller is reading from his notes.

Making Contact

"I like to say hello the moment the telephone is answered," says Bill Miller, a seventeen-year sales veteran and president of his own company that sells perishable tools and capital equipment for gear production. He believes success in cold-call selling comes from being sincere, articulate, and respectful. "You must have a good, strong voice," he says, "and respect your contact's time."

Being clear about the goal of your call is something successful salespeople know and make their number one priority. Whether your mission is to set up a future meeting, send company literature, or just introduce your goods and services, you must know that every word counts, and on the telephone you have no time to make mistakes.

Having been connected with your prospective customer, you'll want to begin with an interesting opening conversation. You might say something like, "Hello Ms. Jones, my name is John Smith and I represent Corporate Appearances Inc. My company specializes in (name the ultimate result your product provides). This might be worth your time to take a look at. I'd like to ask you some questions just to see whether you'd like more information."

Listen attentively and make short notes during the course of the conversation, making sure that doing so doesn't interfere with your attention to what your contact is saying. When you have your contact's ear, continue to ask open-ended questions.

Again, be direct by inquiring about the basics: Who is responsible for buying this product, and how do they handle it? Direct questions show you are in control of the conversation and you know what you're doing. Avoid using weak language, such as, "I wonder if you could . . ." or "I'm just trying to find out about. . . ." These kinds of statements do not represent authority. Instead they say very clearly to your prospective customer that you lack confidence in your sales abilities.

If your contact is busy, respect her time and ask whether you can call back at a more convenient time. Asking permission to carry on the conversation by inquiring if it is a good time to talk makes a good impression and shows the other person that you are polite and respectful. Set a future date and time and then make sure to follow up.

Although some people suggest going right for the appointment setting, most professionals realize their prospective customer may either not be interested immediately or want to think things through before going further. Says one twenty-year sales pro, "If my prospect is qualified and he seems to have some interest, I can use the remaining time to pique his curiosity over the phone and pre-sell him on what we'll talk further about in an upcoming meeting."

An example of this might be to say, "Mr. Kent, based on what you've told me, it looks like I could show you several ways to save with our program. The best thing to do might be for us to get together so I can ask you a few more questions and show you some of the options we have available to see if what we can offer is a good fit. How about some time next week?"

Never ask for a decision in the opening of a cold call or say something such as "I'd like to stop by on Monday at noon, or would 3:00 P.M. be better?" You'll find your customer will most often be resistant to making such on-the-spot plans about something he knows little or nothing about.

Likewise, don't send information before you call unless it is a well-designed business card that serves as a future calling card. Busy executives and decision makers usually toss unsolicited literature with form letters. Beginning your call by saying, "Did you get the information I sent you last week?" is not the way to get new and continuing business. It would be one in a thousand at best who would answer with "Yes! When shall we set up a meeting?"

Don't let a "not interested" reply get you down. The next call you make has nothing to do with the one or more you've completed that didn't get a positive reaction. Letting negative thoughts in will affect your entire attitude.

Instead of setting your goal for a sale, perhaps look at a secondary goal not as steep and more attainable. Simply making a call and identifying someone as a prospective customer, for example, will make you feel more successful and keep you moving forward. And it's much more productive than avoiding the phone and walking about hoping things will automatically change.

"No" doesn't mean "no." It means "no, not today."

"No" doesn't necessarily mean the prospect doesn't like or want your product. It often indicates that the timing is not right, or there's an unspoken objection. Here are some techniques to help you deal with "no" more effectively:

- *Be prepared for "no."* After all, most people say "no" a lot more often than they say "yes." So why stutter and fume when your current prospect says no, as if you've never heard it before? Treat it as a problem to be solved, not a personal rejection.

- *Ask and answer questions.* Instead of looking at "no" as the final chapter in your business relationship, ask questions and be prepared to answer some yourself. You may discover alternative solutions.

- *Control your feelings.* As a professional, you're probably not going to stomp your feet, but if you appear defensive or desperate, it might not be much better. Avoid accusatory comments and sarcasm.

- *Take some time.* You don't have to resolve the issues surrounding "no" right that minute. It may be good for both sides to take a couple of days to think things over.

- *Follow up.* Stay in touch with the customer consistently. There could still be ways you can help each other, even if you don't actually do business together right away.

- *Don't be pushy.* Once everything has been said, let it settle in on both sides. The customer may not want to hear from you for a while for whatever reasons. Respect that, and the customer will see you as a professional.

This is not an original observation, but if you are not hearing "no" frequently, you are doomed to failure as a salesperson. Reason: the majority of people you talk to—about anything, from selling a prospect to asking for a date—are going to say "no."

Let's say the ratio of "no" to "yes" is 9 to 1, meaning you will close 10 percent of your sales, and not sell to 90 percent of those you talk to. By logical extension, you are going to hear nine "no's" for every one "yes."

Therefore, if you never hear "no," it means you are not asking potential customers whether they will buy from you. This lack of sales activity may insulate you from rejection, but statistically, it will never get you to the level of "yes's" you need to earn a good living in sales.

ATTRACTION PRINCIPLE #10:

Don't agonize over a rejection. Move on to the next call.

A wise man once said, "It's not what happens to you; it's how you handle it."

Sure, it hurts when a big sale you thought you had in the bag suddenly flies apart. But get over it. Grieve quickly, then move to the next opportunity even faster. Whenever a door closes in one place, one usually opens in another. Find the next open door.

On the other hand, it certainly is helpful to know why you did not get the sale. Was your price too high? Were you too aggressive? Was the competitor's warranty better than yours? These are things you need to know.

When you lose the sale, ask the prospect: "Would you mind telling me why we didn't get the order?" You can ask this in person, over the phone, or by e-mail, depending on your comfort level.

Never show anger that you were not picked. And when the prospect tells you whom she did buy from, never say anything negative about that supplier. When you criticize the prospect's purchase decision, you insult their intelligence and also make them feel bad. Their reaction is anger. They assume that your negative assessment of their purchase is driven by your selfish motive to get the order, and is not honest, objective advice.

> Instead, if at all possible, be positive (as long as you are being honest): "They are a great company; you are in very good hands."

The prospect expects salespeople to become angry when they are rejected and to badmouth whatever company beat them out for the contract. Doing the opposite surprises the prospect in a positive way: She has heard so many salespeople badmouth competitors, that when you are complimentary, it creates a positive impression that can lead to future opportunities for you.

The Follow-Up Letter

At the end of the conversation, summarize what's been talked about. Highlight your important points and be very clear about the time and the date of your next step. Thank your contact for his time and interest before ending your call. Make sure you send a written note or e-mail as soon as possible.

In this correspondence, you'll again cover the important points and restate the next steps and time and date for your next conversation. Include information about the current company's situation, what needs and problems are occurring, and how your product or service can resolve it. This summary will help you move one step further toward the close of your sale. You and your customer now have—in writing—what was said throughout your conversation and are clear about what will happen next.

ATTRACTION PRINCIPLE #11:

Keep the pipeline filled, and you won't have to worry about running out of water.

Do you spend your time fighting and arguing with marginal prospects because you don't have inquiries from serious buyers? Then you're not prospecting enough and generating enough leads. As the late Paul Bringe once observed: "When the feed is scarce, the chickens will scratch at anything."

The solution is to generate more inquiries. When you have more prospects than you can handle, you can afford to be more selective. Are you using direct mail, the Internet, the telephone, networking, advertising, referrals, trade shows, and the other proven prospecting methods to keep your pipeline filled?

When you have many more potential opportunities for business than you need, you can be more selective in those you pursue. As a result, you follow up only with those leads who are the best fit for you. The greater compatibility and confidence makes you more attractive to these prospects.

On the other hand, if you have a shortage of inquiries, and your lead pipeline is empty, you may feel desperate about your immediate prospects for future sales. This desperation comes across to prospects, making you far less attractive.

Market your products and services even when you already have more customers than you can handle. At that stage, you market not to get business; you market to have a choice: to be able to pick and choose the customers you want to work with. When the demand for your product or service consistently outweighs the supply, people become aware of it, and this makes you even more in demand and attractive to them.

Note

1. Ron Fielding, personal communication.

Magnetic Follow-Up

Most salespeople dread following up on leads because they fear they will come across as pestering the prospect. This chapter reveals five follow-up techniques that work and dozens of follow-up phrases that will help warm up the prospects and make them welcome and look forward to hearing from you—and eliminate concerns that you are calling them too often.

Follow-Up Can Be Frustrating

Don't you hate it when a prospect calls with a (supposedly) urgent need? You drop everything to do an estimate, you begin to clear your schedule to make room for this new project, you submit your proposal, and then you wait. And you wait. When you don't hear back, you call to follow up and they say they haven't had time to look at your proposal yet. You wait some more and, though you dread it, you call again. Or maybe you don't. In any case, you never hear from them again.

This happens all the time—not just to you—and there's little you can do about it, except try to see it from the other side. Here's what it may look like from your prospect's perspective.

On the day they called you, this project was at the top of their list; the next day, something else came along that took priority and kept pushing the project further and further away, until it was on a permanent back burner. They never bothered to let you know, probably because they got caught up in their own world. It happens to all of us.

So here's a little reality check for difficult follow-up moments:

What they say:	I have a project. Could you send your information?
What you hear:	They want me.
What they mean:	They're gathering information.
What to do:	Send your info. Follow up in a week.
What they say:	Your info is here somewhere but I haven't looked at it yet.
What you hear:	They chose someone else.
What they mean:	Other things have come up and the project isn't quite as urgent.
What to do:	Ask when to call back. Keep in touch.
What they say:	Your materials look interesting, but we haven't decided what direction to take. We'll be in touch.
What you hear:	They chose someone else.
What they mean:	Things have changed. The project is not a priority.
What to do:	Keep in touch quarterly for other possible projects.
What they say:	Nothing. No call back.
What you hear:	They chose someone else.
What they mean:	They're busy with other things or maybe they did choose someone else. It's not the end of the world.
What to do:	Keep in touch every few months by e-mail, mail, and phone.

Five Follow-Up Techniques That Work

"I've got someone who could use your help," a colleague told me. "She heads up a software company that needs to promote its product better. I told her you'd get in touch." My colleague handed me her contact information.

I e-mailed. No reply. I followed up with a phone call. And I still haven't heard back. Not a peep. And this is someone who needed—and asked for—my help.

An isolated case? Hardly. Last month, I submitted a proposal to a prospect to revamp his website. He was very excited about the project—but every time I try to reach him to get a "yes" or a "no," all I get is silence. He too "should" have responded . . . but he hasn't.

When this happens, it's annoying. But that doesn't necessarily mean you're being ignored. These days, it seems to be the way more and more very busy people are simply saying, "Not right now."

So what do you do about it? Do you leave the ball in their court and just sit around waiting for them to hit it back? Of course not.

It takes an average of five to seven sales calls to close a deal. So if you always give up after the first couple of tries, you'll never sell your service to anyone. It's your responsibility to remind your prospects (sometimes again and again) that they are interested in your proposal. It's your responsibility to be persistent until they're ready to continue the conversation.

That said, here are five tried-and-true techniques you can use to speed up the process:

1. *Ask for a simple "yes" or "no."* Author and physician Evan Lipkis got silence from a reporter from *Lady's Home Journal* after submitting an article idea. So he wrote a simple e-mail message that said, "Just give me a yes or no!" He got a 40-minute interview and a story in the magazine.

2. *Put "Second Request" in the e-mail subject line.* When faced with silence, Howard Stone, co-author of *Too Young to Retire*, sends the same e-mail message a week later with "Second Request" in the subject line.

3. *Give them a deadline to respond.* Some people only take action when a deadline is looming. So ask your prospects to respond by a certain date, even if that date is arbitrary.

4. *Express concern.* On a second or third try, express concern by saying "I hope you are all right." This works especially well with people you know

personally. It brings the interaction to a human level, reminds them that there's a real person trying to reach them, and usually provokes a response.

5. *Put them on auto-drip.* Whether or not you have a deal pending, you should have an automated marketing tool in place to help keep your name in all your prospects' minds. The three best ways to remind them of the service that you provide are with a monthly (or even quarterly) e-mail newsletter, a print newsletter, or a direct-mail postcard.

I know what you're thinking. You don't want to be a pest. So where is that line between pestiness and persistence?

There is no definite answer. It will be different for every prospect. But it will help you stay on the right side of the line by asking them questions like, "When should I contact you next?" and "Do you mind if I stay in touch every month or so?"

And remember this: When they're ready to go ahead with your proposal, they will be grateful that you didn't give up. In fact, the next time you call, they just might say, "I'm so glad to hear from you. I've been meaning to call."

Are You Being a Pest?

Follow-up is essential, but exactly how to follow up is the real work of marketing. When pursuing a prospect, you may wonder just how hard to push. You don't want to be perceived as a pest, but when you get no response, it's easy to go crazy imagining all kinds of things. So how do you know what to do?

There are no rules, of course, but when in doubt, err on the side of too much contact, rather than too little, or else you'll never know what opportunities you missed. Go with your gut, not your paranoia. And use these follow-up guidelines:

1. Ask if it's a good time to talk, always. If they say no, respect that. Don't try to give a shortened spiel.
2. Tell them how you found them. People will become instantly more receptive if, in a letter or on the phone, you begin by saying, "I got your name from. . . ."

3. Ask if they want you to call back and, if so, find out when is the best time to talk. If you sense they're just saying "yes" to get off the phone, ask if it's really worth your time and theirs to pursue the relationship.

4. Wait until they're ready to listen to you. Otherwise you'll waste your breath.

5. Listen to their response. That's the key. Just because you place the call doesn't mean you have to do all the talking.

6. Know when "no" means NO, and let it go.

When Is It Too Late to Follow Up?

You know those people you met recently but haven't followed up with yet? Well, what are you waiting for?! Do you realize that follow up is more important than attending an event? Why? Because, if you don't keep in touch with a few of the prospects and colleagues you meet, you've wasted your time by going (well, almost).

Many salespeople ask, "When is it too late to follow up?" The answer is: never. The amount of time that has passed will simply determine what you say and how you say it. (If it's been a while, you'll need to remind them who you are and what you talked about). Here are four guidelines that can help:

1. *Ask for something.* Send an email message to everyone whose card you collected at a recent event. But go beyond "nice to meet you" and ask for help or a resource for a project you're working on—personal or professional. This can get a dialogue going between you.

2. *Offer to meet or talk on the phone.* In particular, choose someone you only exchanged cards with (but didn't get a chance to talk to for long) and invite them for coffee or to view each other's work.

3. *Get them in your loop.* If you have a newsletter (or even a semi-regular snail mail campaign), ask if you can keep in touch by adding them to your list (and tell them what they'll get).

4. *Get more involved.* If you liked the event and want to get more in-

volved with the group, follow up with one of the organizers and ask what kind of help they need.

Ask a Question to Jump-Start a Stalled Sale

It can be discouraging when you call and e-mail (and call and e-mail some more) the prospects you want to work with and they just don't respond. They may be so inundated that they can only respond to what's urgent or at the top of their "to do" list.

But you could probably also make it easier for them to respond. One technique that works is to ask one simple question. For example, when you give your short introduction (via e-mail or voice mail), do you ask your prospect directly whether they are open to working with companies like yours?

Simple questions like that one can often spur action. Here are some other examples of simple questions you can ask:

- Do you work with outside design firms? (or fill in the blank with whatever you do).
- Are you the right contact or is there someone else I should be talking to about (fill in the blank)?
- Would you like to receive our tips about (blank) via e-mail?
- Did you see the article in (blank) in which you are featured? (That's good for prospects you find in the press.)
- Did you see the piece in our portfolio that we did for (fill in with their competition)? We'd love to tell you more about that project. (This is good for follow-up calls.)

Again, I'm not suggesting you use all of these questions, just one (or maybe two at the most). If you're successful, you'll have time to ask the others later.

Remember: The goal of an introduction is to find out whether they are open to speaking with you, either now or at some point in the future. If you ask them, they will often tell you.

Follow Up Immediately via E-Mail

After an initial conversation with a prospect, whether you called them or they called you, don't wait to start your follow-up. That same day, build on the momentum of your freshness in their mind by sending an e-mail message in which you:

1. Thank them for their interest, for taking the time to speak with you, for visiting your website, or anything else they went out of their way to do.

2. Express what you understand to be the challenge they face. Use as many of the words they used as you can.

3. Refer to an experience or project in your background that supports your claim that you are the right resource to help them.

4. Provide a link to your website and, in particular, a case study or article that is most relevant, based on what you know so far about their challenge.

If too much time passes before you follow up, sometimes even a day or two, the conversation may slip into the recesses of their mind, or blur with that of others like you, and therefore won't make as strong of an impact.

Ten Powerful Follow-Up Questions

When following up on the phone, here are a few opening questions that can get the conversation started:

1. "Am I catching you at a bad time?"
2. "Did you receive the information I sent you?"
3. "Did you have a chance to look over the material?"
4. "Do you use this type of product or service from time to time?"
5. "Do you have a budget for acquiring this product or service?"
6. "What is the approximate amount of the budget?"
7. "What's your time frame for acquiring this type of product: three months, six months, longer?"

8. "Are you authorized to approve this purchase, or will others be involved in the approval?"

9. "Is there anything I should have asked you that I haven't?"

10. "What do you want to happen next?"

And when making follow-up contacts, these phrases can help warm up the prospect and set the right tone:

- "Thanks for speaking to me (or meeting with me)."
- "I know your time is valuable."
- "As we discussed . . ."
- "I look forward to continuing our conversation."
- "Call me with any questions."
- "Call me to continue the conversation."
- "Let me know if I can be of any help."
- "We haven't spoken in a while and I wanted to check in and see if anything has changed. . . ."
- "Perhaps you are in a better position than when we first spoke to use our products/services."
- "I was wondering if you are still planning to buy these products/ services?"

Following Up with Nonresponders via Fax

There is an unfortunate tendency in business today not to return calls—especially from salespeople. What can you do?

One method is to send a short fax. It tells the prospect, "I've been trying to reach you without success. Please indicate your preference below."

Then have a series of check-off boxes the prospect can check and fax back to you. They read something like:

[ ] I've just been very busy. Try me on (date) _____.

[ ] Now is not the right time. Try me on (date) _____.

[ ] I'm no longer interested because (please give reason) _____

_____.

Many prospects who may be ducking your phone calls will respond to this low-pressure fax inquiry. If they check one of the first two boxes, call back on the date specified. If they check the last box, and the reason they give as to why they are no longer interested is an objection you can overcome, call or fax a reply.

Should You Pursue All of Your Leads?

Before you decide to pursue a piece of business, ask yourself these questions:

- Do the prospect's needs match the capabilities that our products and services provide?
- What company resources will be spent to win this business? Can we afford it? Is it worth it?
- Is the prospect willing to give us an equal opportunity to compete for their business? Is the playing field truly level, or are we just being used as a second bid?

The reality is you can't control your prospects, and it's almost impossible to know in advance whether a lead is a good one or whether the project you're quoting will go anywhere. On first impression, you can't always tell the literature collectors from the bona fide prospects. Sometimes you may want to say, "Tell me either yes or no, but don't keep me hanging on like this." But they can't. Only time will tell.

What you can control is how you spend your time. And you decide how vigorously you want to pursue each project and how much time you can afford to devote to each prospect. In order to do that, you have to rate your prospects and prioritize your efforts toward them.

Inquiry Fulfillment for Prospects Who Have an Immediate Need

To satisfy anyone's urgent need, have the basic information about your products or services ready and faxable (three pages maximum). Then, if necessary, take your time to put together a more tailored package and mail it. Even better, post this literature on your website. That way, prospects can access it at any time of the day or night.

When you promise to send information, be sure to send it promptly. Sloppy lead handling looks really bad, and, as marketing consultant David Wood writes:

Failure to fulfill your first commitment to a customer establishes you as unreliable and undependable. In addition, the sooner your material gets there, the fresher your conversation is in his or her mind and the more quickly your relationship can be continued.

More Follow-Up Strategies That Work

As we've noted, people today rarely return phone calls. It's unprofessional, but it's a reality. So now, more than ever, it's up to you to follow up.

For qualified leads (e.g., hot prospects—especially those who've contacted you) follow-up calls make sense. The call should be made approximately a week after the information is sent out, on any day but Monday.

For cold prospects (e.g., people who don't know you), follow-up calls can only help. It's unrealistic to think that you could do follow-up calls to everyone on your calling list, but you could certainly make calls to the top 10 percent of potential customers on the list.

Chances are they got your mail and it's in a pile somewhere. Your phone call will resurrect your piece of paper from that pile and, because timing is everything in marketing, that follow-up call could provide the final push needed to get the project on track. A prospect might surprise you with, "You know, I've been meaning to call you."

From the time you make your first contact with the prospects, until the time they are ready to buy from you, these follow-up activities are all effective:

- Make a follow-up phone call.
- Send an e-mail.
- Fax a note.
- Send a birthday or holiday card.
- Send articles of interest.
- Send any publicity you get.
- Send a short note or postcard inviting them to check out a new item or function on your website.
- Jot down any ideas relating to their project.

When making the initial follow-up contact, these phrases can help warm up the prospect and set the right tone:

- "Thanks for speaking to me (or meeting with me)."
- "I know your time is valuable."
- "As we discussed. . . ."
- "I look forward to continuing our conversation."
- "Call me with any questions."
- "Call me to continue the conversation."
- "Let me know if I can be of any help."

For subsequent follow-up phone calls, the following phrases may also be helpful:

- "We haven't spoken in a while and I wanted to check in and see if anything has changed."
- "Perhaps you are in a better position to use our services than when we first spoke."
- "I was wondering whether you are still planning to buy these services."

Here are some additional tips and thoughts about following up:

- Following up is marketing to the same group over and over.
- Don't forget to follow up with your former customers.
- Make follow-up letters brief. Use a Post-it Note.
- They're just reminders, to jog memories.
- Always call to make sure your information was received.
- Capture their e-mail addresses. Send periodic short items of interest to them over the Internet.

Ranking Prospects for Follow-Up

You can't follow up with everyone and the good news is, you don't have to. But in order to decide whom to pursue and whom to let go, you have to determine their value to you—qualify them, in marketing lingo.

The big question: Is there a fit? Don't be so eager to get a project that you fail to consider a prospect's fitness for you. Exhibit 8-1 presents a checklist of questions to consider about each prospect to help you assign a rating: A, B, C or Hot, Warm, Cold—whatever labels work for you. The key point: Not every prospect should be followed up. And not all prospects should be given an equal follow-up effort. Spend the most time and effort following up with your hot prospects. Give others only occasional reminders of your existence.

Measuring Results

"I don't like to assess success simply by measuring response," says Ilise Benun, publisher of *The Art of Self Promotion* quarterly newsletter:

> There are too many unknowns that figure into the ultimate results. This is a lesson I've learned many times, but I'll never forget one time several years ago. I spoke at a conference that was very poorly publicized and, thus, poorly attended. My workshop had five people. I spontaneously changed the format of my presentation, put us into an intimate circle and gave a highly interactive self-promotion workshop (which I wouldn't

EXHIBIT 8-1. RATE YOUR PROSPECTS.

Business Potential

_____ 1. Why aren't they still working with their previous vendor?

_____ 2. Do they have future needs? Immediate needs?

_____ 3. Is there potential for ongoing business?

The Decision-Making Process

_____ 1. Is your contact the decision maker?

_____ 2. Are there several layers of bureaucracy to deal with?

_____ 3. Can they afford you?

_____ 4. Can they pay a percentage of your fee up front?

Personality/Working Style

_____ 1. Does your contact respect your time and labor?

_____ 2. Do they require a lot of hand-holding?

_____ 3. Do they understand that you have other clients?

_____ 4. Do they buy based on price? Quality? Both?

_____ 5. Do they respect your professional boundaries?

_____ 6. Do they do business honestly and with integrity?

_____ 7. Do you feel comfortable with them?

Your Fitness for Them

_____ 1. Does this project fit into your specialty?

_____ 2. Could you refer someone who would be a better fit?

_____ 3. Do they require more time, service, or technical expertise than you have available?

Once you've given each prospect a rating, determine your strategy. Here's a sample rating system and strategy.

HOT—Has an immediate need. Follow up right away.

WARM—Will have a need soon. Ask how they want you to follow up.

COOL—May have future needs. Keep on the mailing list and contact quarterly.

COLD—Worth one call to see that they received information. Otherwise, let them come to you.

have been able to do with a big group). It turned out to be extremely productive and everyone left feeling great, myself included. If asked the next day how many people showed up, the number five would have drawn a groan from anyone. But more is not always better—and it wasn't that day. A year later, one of those five became an important customer for me.[1]

Of course, response is important. But while response is indeed significant, it's not everything. It's difficult to imagine that those who receive phone calls but don't respond are affected in a positive way. But don't assume they're not.

There are too many unknowns. People's needs and interests are constantly changing. You'll never know, for example, how many people put your brochure in that infamous "in-basket," which they really do plan to go through just as soon as they get a free minute.

You'll never know how many people file your material for future use, or bookmark your website for future reference. You'll never know how many people pass your catalog along to a colleague who may be calling soon. You'll never know how many people are presenting the idea of working with you to their bosses but haven't yet received approval.

Yes, they're intangible and unquantifiable, but all of these events can have an impact on the results of your promotional efforts, and you'll never be able to trace them back to any one mailing.

But you have to measure something. You need some way to know if what you're doing is working—a gauge by which to judge. If you need some hard facts, go ahead and measure response. Make 500 calls. Count how many people respond positively, and keep track of how many jobs result from that one phone effort. Just keep in mind that it's not the whole picture.

Give each marketing effort six months, minimum. More often than not, it's not just one communication that brings a customer; it's the succession of messages. It can take four to nine calls to make a sale.

When you do make a judgment, take a wide view and go with your gut. You will know whether what you're doing is worth the time and energy involved. You will know whether you enjoy the process. You will know whether people like it, remember it, and notice it. You will know whether, over the course of a year of consistent marketing, your business has grown.

Timing

How often should you follow up? There's no set formula, only some guidelines. A good starting point is the "Rule of Seven," formulated by marketing expert Dr. Jeffrey Lant. It states that to penetrate the buyer's consciousness and make significant penetration in a given market, you have to contact those people a minimum of seven times within an eighteen-month period.

This is slightly more than once every quarter. Although your frequency may be less or more, seven contacts within eighteen months—or four to five contacts within a year—is a good starting point for a follow-up plan.

You can modify this plan to suit your preferences. It's really up to you. Do what works. Don't get locked into a formula. If you get better results contacting warm prospects monthly, do so . . . as long as you keep below a frequency they will find annoying or offensive.

How do you know whether you are following up too frequently? If only one or two prospects complain or seem annoyed, just modify your schedule to accommodate them. But if 5 percent or more respond negatively to your frequency of follow-up, scale back on follow-up for that entire group of prospects. Use prospects' feedback to guide you in your efforts.

When you follow up, you will often encounter prospects with an attitude. That attitude may be positive and friendly. But more often, it is reserved, guarded, or adversarial. Here are some ideas for handling these different situations.

Calling and Finding the Prospect Friendly or Receptive

Here's a rare thrill: You call and the prospect actually seems happy to hear from you again! Don't get excited or interpret levels of commitment and enthusiasm that may not be there. Some people are naturally effervescent and outgoing, yet may not have the slightest interest in dealing with you. Others who are stony and silent may surprise you with an order.

When the prospects are friendly or receptive, match their enthusiasm, but don't exceed it. Prospects resent it when salespeople misinterpret friendliness as interest or commitment. They resent being pushed to a place they are not ready to go. Mirror the prospects' levels of energy, but let their responses guide you. Don't push to close a sale or set an appointment until you get signals they're ready to do so.

If you are not certain whether the prospects are ready to take action, during a lull in the conversation or toward the end, ask, "What's the next step?" or "What do you want to happen next?" If the prospects want to buy, they'll tell you what they need next from you to make a buying decision. Provide it.

Certainly you should always seek to get to the next step in the buying process. Push the prospect, but do it gently. Don't rush prospects, because it doesn't work, and often backfires.

Many salespeople try to achieve a different next step than the prospect seeks. It's okay to try to do what you want as well as what they want. But don't ignore or refuse prospects' requests.

One sales training institution teaches its students, "Never send literature, even if the prospect asks for it." This is ridiculous. Can you imagine calling up a company, asking for a brochure, and being told, "No, we can't send one." Can you imagine your prospects' reaction if you said this to them? It's absurd.

Calling and Finding the Prospect Neutral or Reserved

More often, the prospects will be slightly cool to you when you call to follow up. This doesn't mean they are not interested. But obviously, if they were ready to buy at that second, they probably would have called you versus you calling them.

You are interrupting their activities to try and sell something. So why be surprised if you receive a reception that's lukewarm at best?

You can do several things to warm up the call. Of course, ask, "Am I catching you at a bad time?" If the prospects seem busy or say they are busy, say, "I understand how busy you are. Do you have three minutes now?" When you tell prospects the entire call will take less than three minutes, they become more comfortable, because they realize you aren't going to try to keep them tied up.

A short conversational exchange on a slightly personal note can help here, too. Comment on the weather, or the World Series, or some other fairly neutral topic. If the prospect makes such a comment, pick up the thread and go with it for half a minute or so.

With contact management software (discussed later in this chapter), you gain the advantage of having all data about the prospects in front of you on a computer screen as you talk. If a prospect mentioned she was going to Hawaii last time you talked, ask her how it was. If she was playing in a golf tournament, ask her how it went. You get the idea.

How long you continue the call depends on whether the prospects warm up. If they get in a chatty mood, keep the conversation going, while steering it toward your objective. If they remain distant or cool, or seem pressed for time, respect that, and keep the call brief. Use your own judgment.

Calling and Finding the Prospect Negative or Unreceptive

"Am I catching you at a bad time?" works well here too. It either gets them to drop the stuffed shirt act and behave in a friendlier fashion, or prompts them to share with you that they are busy, in which case, you set a time for a call back.

Do not assume there is something wrong when a prospect seems distant or cold. He may be busy, under pressure, or working against a deadline. Maybe his wife is divorcing him, his sales are lousy, his child is ill, or he has lost his biggest customer. A poor reception doesn't mean there is an objection to you or your call. It just means now is not the best time. If that's the case, the best move is to find out when is the best time . . . and call back then.

Calling and Getting Blocked by the Assistant or Gatekeeper

The last two times you called you reached the prospect, no problem. But now you can't reach him. Instead, you always get a secretary or receptionist.

Again, this doesn't mean the prospect is deliberately ducking your calls, although if he is busy or not ready to buy, that may be the case. It usually means he has someone else picking up the phone because he is too busy to talk to anyone—not that he is singling you out for special treatment because you're a salesperson.

One of the most common screening questions is, "Is she expecting your call?" If the callback is scheduled, the answer is easy—"Yes, we had an appointment to talk today at this time"—and will often bypass the secretarial blockade.

In my office, we have an even better technique: We include each secretary's or assistant's name in our sales database. And we consider them as a first contact rather than a barrier to overcome.

Therefore, instead of trying to fool secretaries or bully our way past them, we talk to them, and make them our allies in reaching their bosses. Some even like us so much, they do some of the selling for us, urging their bosses to buy from us instead of the other suppliers who treat secretaries like second-class citizens.

When an assistant helps us reach the boss, we often reward them with a nice box of gift chocolates sent Federal Express. You have no idea how effectively this puts the assistant on our side.

Calling and Being Told, "We're Looking at Other Suppliers"

The critical issue is not whether they are interviewing other people, but whether they have made a decision to choose someone else and have made a commitment to do business with that supplier.

If they have, you're probably sunk—for now. But keep in touch. The vendor they've chosen may not work out. Or the prospect may have additional needs. Use follow-ups to remind them you are available.

When prospects choose someone else, don't sulk. Don't tell prospects they made a mistake or try to hunt for weakness in the other suppliers' credentials. The decision is already made. If you say they made a bad one— even if you believe it—they'll get angry. No one likes hearing that.

People want to believe they made the right choice. Once a choice is made, they want it praised. Not damned. So when your prospects choose a competitor, congratulate them. Say they made a good choice and should be happy. This creates a favorable impression.

Then gently remind them you're available if additional needs arise. This leaves the door open to future business. Never criticize or degrade the prospects' decisions. Why burn bridges?

If the prospects haven't made a decision yet, say: "Will you do me a favor? Before you make your final selection, call me, and let's talk briefly . . . whether we're the firm you select or not."

The purpose? To give you a chance to talk with the prospects one last time before the decision is made. If you reach the prospects before they have committed to someone else, there's still a chance of getting the business. On the other hand, if the next time you talk with the prospects, the choices have already been made, there's little to zero chance of changing the prospects' minds—at least for the time being.

Calling and Being Told, "We've Looked It Over and We're Not Interested"

Again, this isn't necessarily a rejection of you. It's possible your service doesn't meet their needs, or the needs have changed or vanished. Still, you want to find out more. Maybe another one of your services would meet the requirements, but your prospects don't even know you sell it.

Or maybe your service still fits their new needs, but you have to help them see it. How do you find out the reason why they're not interested? One way is to be direct: "When we last spoke, you seemed very interested. I'm curious. What happened?"

Another way is to act as if the selling part of the conversation is over because they told you they're not buying—and get them to confide in you. Say, "I understand I'm not going to sell you anything today. And I'm going to take your name out of our prospect database so we don't bother you any more. But now that it's over, let me ask: What did we do wrong? What could we have done differently to get you to say yes?" Often the prospects will reveal the real objections, which, once in the open, can sometimes be overcome.

ATTRACTION PRINCIPLE #12:

Sometimes you won't get the order no matter what you do. Prospects will like you more if you don't act like them not ordering is the end of the world.

"The more I live, the more I don't always get what I want," writes best-selling author Robert B. Parker in his book *Hush Money*.

In baseball, a hitter who gets a hit one out of four times at bat is average. A player who gets a hit one out of three times at bat is a superstar.

You're not going to get a hit every time or even most of the time. Babe Ruth got more home runs than any other player of his day, but also more strikeouts. Concentrate on the hits you do get, and don't fret about the pitches you miss.

It's the same in sales: Celebrate the ones you win, and quickly let go of the ones you don't. When you stew over rejection, it causes a negative feeling, and that vibe is transmitted to everyone you talk with throughout that day.

Salespeople who appear to have the customer's best interests at heart are magnetically attractive to their prospects. Conversely, salespeople who act as if they should—and have to—close every sale, regardless of whether doing so is in the best interests of the customer, have the opposite effect: Prospects sense their selfish concerns and are repelled.

Keeping Track of Prospects

If none of your prospects fell through the cracks, isn't it just possible that you'd have enough business? Fewer people would be so frantic about getting new business if they were on top of all the leads that came their way, responded promptly to requests for information, and followed them all the way through.

Call it apathy or just plain disorganization, but without proper management, leads and referrals fall through the cracks and, alas, much business is lost. Often it's the details that prevent you from following up. To do it properly, you must have everything in one place: phone numbers, notes from previous conversations, price quotes.

You can use a manual system, such as a hanging file or a three-ring binder, but that will only work if you remember to open them. Other manual systems include appointment books, wall schedulers, calendars, three-ring notebooks, hanging files organized by month and day, and index cards in recipe file boxes.

In theory, these systems are simple. You note all relevant information about the prospect on their index card or a piece of paper. Each prospect is on a separate card or sheet. Cards and sheets are filed not alphabetically, but according to when the next follow-up call is to take place.

This works. But there are drawbacks. As the number of prospects and customers in your sales database grows, paper systems become cumbersome: There are too many cards, too many sheets, too many files to deal with. Also, the paper files can only be retrieved according to the way they are organized, which is by call-back date. If you want to look up information on a prospect, you won't be able to find his file unless you are lucky enough to remember the call-back date.

The computer solves these problems. Put your sales database on your computer. You can use software to schedule follow-up calls. But at the same time, you can instantly retrieve any file by customer name, company name, state, or whatever other criteria you choose. Now prospect files don't get lost, and vital information is always just a click of the mouse away.

Today, of course, there are loads of software packages to help you do what is called contact management. My intention here is not to review software programs but merely to tell you how easy ACT! and TeleMagic for Windows can make follow-up. (I can't compare them to other packages because they are the only ones we've ever used in my office.)

I can tell you that when we turn on the computer in the morning (because I've already scheduled the tasks), the information is all right there and all we have to do is make the calls. Nothing falls through the cracks.

The program tells us who we have to call that day, what we discussed last time, the date we last spoke with them, the topic of today's conversation, and even what time to call them! It all comes up on your screen automatically, so you don't miss follow-ups you promised to make.

You don't have to buy contact management software to track prospects and sales on your computer. You can buy a database program and design your own custom system. But with so many good contact management programs on the market at prices ranging from $95 to $600, I'd recommend investing in one and learning how to use it.

Whether you are shopping for a contact management program (they are sometimes called "sales database programs" or "personal information managers") or planning to design your own, the software should be able to capture the following information for each prospect:

- Name
- Title
- Company
- Business phone number
- Home phone number
- E-mail address
- Website
- Fax number
- Street address
- City
- State
- Zip code
- Country
- Source of inquiry (how they found out about you)
- Date of inquiry
- Description of their product or service requirements
- A record of follow-ups (dates and discussion summaries)
- The date for the next follow-up call

The software should have the following capabilities:

- Retrieve any prospect file by company name
- Retrieve any prospect file by prospect name
- Automatically schedule follow-up calls
- Keep track of prospect contacts
- Print a complete list of prospects with company names, addresses, and phone numbers
- Sort and print prospect lists by alphabetical order, city, state, zip code, or other criteria you specify

Additional capabilities that are nice to have but not a necessity include:

- Form and custom sales letters
- Generation of quotes and proposals
- Online product literature or fact sheets
- Mail-merge for sending out direct mailings
- Automatic dial-up of prospects' phone numbers
- Compatibility with other software applications

Note

1. Ilise Benun, "Follow-Up Strategies," www.marketing-mentor.com.

CHAPTER 9

Magnetic Sales Presentations

Okay. You've identified the prospect—the real decision maker. And you've convinced him or her to see you. Now here's where the rubber meets the road: you get to come in (or arrange a teleconference) and give your sales presentation.

Here are a few tips for making sure you pull it off and make the impression you want to convey:

1. *Tailor your talk.* Listen to your prospect and tailor your speech accordingly. For instance, if he talks slowly, slow down.

2. *Position yourself.* It's usually best to take a seat near your prospect with nothing standing between the two of you. When you do this, the prospect feels you are on his side. Don't slouch or you'll look disinterested.

3. *Keep good eye contact.* Being able to look somebody in the eye is a sign of confidence that shows you believe in yourself and what you're selling.

4. *Look professional.* The first impression you make with somebody is often a lasting impression.

5. *Let the prospect win at the beginning of the visit.* Agree with the prospect on some minor points (e.g., the weather is too hot). Give the appearance of being easygoing.

6. *Be positive and upbeat.* Taking too seriously something a prospect or customer said causes a negative attitude. A salesperson not sold on himself will feel personally rejected when the sale is not made.

7. *Service the customer.* The best salespeople succeed because they go the extra mile to please their customers. Top salespeople consistently make sure their customers get what they want.

Overcoming Buyer Skepticism

Whenever the buyer expresses doubt about your product or service, use a proof statement. A *proof statement* is a statement containing facts, figures, testimonials, parallel circumstances, expert opinions from someone who does not have a direct involvement in your transaction, or anything else that is tangible, quantifiable, and real. It is the opposite of puffery.

The proof statement is constructed in the following fashion:

- State the benefit you are about to prove.
- Prove the benefit for the buyer using facts, figures, or other tangible information.
- Apply the benefit to the buyer.

Here is an example of a proof statement:

"Ms. Smith, you will find that the new All American Widget will save you time. (State the benefit.) In efficiency studies performed by the National Widget Institute, the All American brand was 16 percent faster to operate for the average employee. (Prove the benefit.) For you, this means employees are more productive and you save that 16 percent for your company. (Apply the benefit.)"

Making Memorable Presentations

If you want to get your message across, it has to be memorable. That's where a "positioning statement" can help cement the unique benefits of your product in the buyer's mind.

The purpose of a *positioning statement* is to create a short message that people will remember. The first sentence tells people what your service is and how they will benefit from it. The second sentence tells how your service is different from that of other firms.

The formula goes like this:

- [Name of firm] is a [category] firm that helps [primary customers] reach [primary benefits].
- Unlike other [category] firms, [name of firm] specializes in [primary difference].

For example:

ABC is an architectural firm that helps medium-sized businesses find and renovate unique commercial spaces. Unlike other architectural firms, ABC specializes in this type of renovation.

Using this simple formula, you can get at the essential description of what your firm does that's different from other firms, and make your message more memorable.

ATTRACTION PRINCIPLE #13:

No one wants a sales call, but everybody looks forward to talking with a friend. Be a friend.

Don't glad-hand, and don't force a relationship. But if there is a connection between you and the prospect, nurture the relationship and let it grow over time. As you move from stranger to account rep, and from account rep to trusted adviser, your effectiveness will multiply greatly over time, resulting in more and easier sales from that account.

Here is a secret for building relationships with customers: give small gifts at unexpected times when they will be most appreciated. Send a box of fine chocolate as a "thank you" for a recent order, to cheer up a customer after a rough patch in her business or personal life, or to say "congratulations" on a special event such as a promotion or the birth of a child or grandchild. I do this routinely and can tell you unequivocally that there are few better—or easier—relationship builders.

But gift-giving, effective though it may be, is a gimmick. The more powerful principle behind it is to actually care about your prospects and customers.

If you are not a "people person," it may be difficult for you to express this caring and communicate it to others. To overcome your reticence, relax and be less stiff. Let more of your natural personality shine through when talking and meeting with other people.

The way to become more at ease and natural with your prospects and customers is to treat business (and life) as what it really is: a game—a fun and stimulating challenge. When you have fun doing your job, you have fun with the people you are doing it with. Your customers will sense this and enjoy being with you.

"People who are likeable, or have what I call a high L-factor, tend to land jobs more easily, find friends more quickly, and have happier relationships," writes Tim Sanders in his book, *The Likeability Factor*. "If you raise your L-factor, you will harness one of life's most powerful forces."

Don't Make a "Presentation"—Have a Conversation

Most people who sell do it absolutely wrong. They follow their own agenda, reciting a memorized list of features and benefits to prospects. But what prospects care about, as copywriter Sig Rosenblum points out, are their needs, problems, concerns, fears, desires, goals, and dreams. Successful salespeople tailor their presentations to show how the features of their product or service can satisfy the prospects' needs and solve their problems.

But how do you find out what prospects want or desire? First and foremost, you listen. Prospects who do not hear what they want to hear from you will tell you so. Usually these statements are in the form of objections.

You may think, "I always listen to prospects and customers." But do you? Be honest. Aren't there times when the prospect is talking and you're not really listening, but instead planning what you want to say next? And when a prospect says something that you don't agree with or don't want to hear, aren't you immediately planning your rebuttal rather than sitting back and listening to see whether the complaint or statement has merit?

Here are some tips for converting your sales meeting from a one-way lecture to a much more productive two-way conversation:

● *Focus.* When you are listening and doing something else at the same time, you aren't really listening. When prospects speak, give them 100 percent of your concentration. If, for instance, you're talking with a prospect over the phone, don't go through your mail at the same time. Follow the advice of poet May Sarton, who said, "Do each thing with absolute concentration." Listening is an active process, not a passive one, and it requires your full attention.

● *Take notes.* Bring a pad and pen to the meeting. As the prospect talks, take notes. There are several benefits to this. First, you can jot down questions as they occur to you, so you don't forget to ask them later on.

Second, you can quickly and easily prepare a good proposal or follow-up letter based on the notes. When you take notes, your follow-up documents will be full of good, specific material prospects want to see, because you recorded their requests and preferences.

Third, the act of note taking is reassuring, visible proof to prospects that you are indeed paying attention to what is being said.

● *Bring a tape recorder.* Ask prospects, "Do you mind if I tape our conversation? I like to make sure I have an accurate record of the information you give me." Most people will readily agree to this. If not, put the recorder away and use a pad and pen to take notes.

I prefer minicassette recorders because they fit easily in a jacket pocket or briefcase, and their smaller size seems less intimidating to prospects. Be sure to bring several extra tapes and spare batteries; I have had batteries die in the middle of a meeting! Also bring a note pad and pen as backup. Some people like to take notes even when recording. They let the recorder capture the conversation, using the pad to jot down questions and key points.

• *Respond verbally.* Say things that indicate to prospects you are listening and have empathy for what they are saying. One simple, effective communication technique for demonstrating your understanding is simply to say, "I understand." For example:

> **Prospect**: "We're looking for a contractor who can handle the job from start to finish. I don't want to have to coordinate and deal with half a dozen or more different vendors. We want one firm to do the whole job."
>
> **You**: "I understand."

Another technique is to rephrase the prospect's statement and repeat it back to her:

> **Prospect**: "We're looking for a contractor who can handle the job from start to finish. I don't want to have to coordinate and deal with half a dozen or more different vendors. We want one firm to do the whole job."
>
> **You**: "So what you're saying is you want a contractor who can provide all the pieces and provide single source responsibility for getting your system designed and installed?"
>
> **Prospect**: "Yes, that's correct."

Equally effective is to rephrase the prospect's statement and repeat it as a question to which he or she will answer affirmatively. This gets the prospect agreeing to things you say, which eventually leads to a close:

> **Prospect**: "We really need an ad campaign that will penetrate the under-thirty market for this product."
>
> **You**: "So would you be interested specifically in dealing with an ad agency with a proven track record in selling to the under-thirty market?"
>
> **Prospect**: "Yes, that's what we're looking for."

Some salespeople are more aggressive, phrasing their question so that the answer indicates a tentative (if small) commitment on the part of the prospect:

Prospect: "We would need seminars to train one hundred staff members no later than the end of February."

You: "So, if we could train your total staff of one hundred by the end of February, you'd be interested in going ahead, wouldn't you?"

● *Respond physically.* "Body language" lets prospects know you are interested and actively involved in the conversation. I like to lean forward slightly, look a prospect in the eyes directly, and nod my head slightly to indicate I am listening and understanding. If you sit back with your arms folded, or stare into space vacantly, the prospect will assume you are not being receptive or attentive.

Listening is such a broad topic that entire books and seminars have been devoted to it, and I can't repeat all that information here. The key is to remember that you are not in the meeting to "give a pitch," as so many salespeople and consultants mistakenly believe, but to help the prospect solve a problem or achieve an objective. You cannot help solve the problem or achieve the objective until you know what it is. And you can't find out what the problem or objective is unless you listen to the prospect.

Also be aware that if you're talking too much, you're listening too little. According to consultant Howard Shenson, when selling your services you should be speaking 40 percent of the time or less, which means you should be listening during at least 60 percent of the conversation.

PROSPECT REPELLANT #8:

Focusing on making the sale rather than solving the prospect's problem.

We discussed in the introduction how prospects are magnetically attracted to salespeople who seem genuinely interested in helping them, rather than driven by their own self-serving motive of closing a sale.

Conversely, prospects are turned off by salespeople who are clearly focused on closing the sale regardless of the circumstances—

especially those who use high-pressure tactics to accomplish this goal.

Probe to Uncover Real Needs

Questions are the single most powerful technique for successfully selling your services to prospects. Questions:

- Demonstrate your concern for the prospect's problems.
- Put the focus where it should be: on the prospect's needs, not your products.
- Enable you to determine the prospect's requirements so you can tailor a solution to address those requirements.

"In the first meeting with the prospective customer, focus on what they really need to make their problem go away," says Howard Shenson. "Don't waste the prospect's time providing a verbal resume. If prospects need information on your skills, abilities, and experience, they will certainly ask."

Often in meetings you go into far more detail about your qualifications, company, industry, methods, or service than prospects care to hear. Many will sit politely because they think it's rude to interrupt; but they are not really listening. Instead, they are eager to get to their agenda. You want to shift the focus to their agenda, not yours, almost immediately. Questions help you do that.

When sitting down with prospects after greetings have been made and pleasantries exchanged, I like to get directly to the reason I'm there. I typically open with a question or request for information, such as "Tell me a little bit about your situation and how I can help you," or "What problem do you have that you'd like me to help you with?" Believe me, this gets them talking.

Here are some other questions I find helpful in getting prospects to open up and tell me how I can help them:

- "Why did you want to get together with me today?"

- "How can I help you?"
- "Tell me a little bit about your current situation."
- "What specifically do you need me to do for you?"
- "What are you looking to accomplish in [name their specific area of interest]?"
- "That's interesting. Can you tell me more?"
- "What did you have in mind?"
- "What do you want to happen next?"

At times, prospects are unable to articulate their requirements and instead go on and on without getting to the point. I help them get back on track by interrupting and saying, "I understand. But what exactly is it that you would like me to do for you?" This usually helps them focus on why they called me in the first place.

If a prospect and I are having a conversation, and I decide to interject a question, I don't jump in and immediately ask it. I pause for a second, then say, "May I ask you a question?" This interruption forces prospects to stop talking, prepares them to listen, and puts them in a receptive, thoughtful state, ensuring that they will hear my question and provide an answer to it. It also says, "I think this is so important that I want us to stop and question what we're talking about so we can proceed on an accurate basis." Use, "May I ask you a question?" It works!

Of course, the point of the sales meeting is not to ask endless questions or gather infinite information. Each question is designed to clarify and diagnose the prospect's requirements, so that you get, as quickly as possible, to the point where you can outline the prospect's project requirements, your proposed plan of action, and your fee.

Show That You Can Solve Their Problem, but Don't Solve It for Free

In the 1980s, sales trainers and authors introduced the concept of consultative selling. Essentially, customers want you to solve problems for them, not "sell" them. Good salespeople aren't peddlers or hucksters; they're sales "consultants" who work closely with customers, helping them fulfill their needs.

Suddenly salespeople in all fields stopped referring to themselves as salespeople and began calling themselves consultants. People who sold financial services, for example, began putting such impressive-sounding titles as "financial planner" or "financial counselor" on their business cards. The consultative salespeople even developed a slogan—"Solve, don't sell"—to push their approach to sales.

Much of the consultative approach to selling is valid. However, in one respect, the consultative selling gurus and disciples went overboard. Some did so much free "consulting" before they were retained by the prospect that they ended up giving away their services, removing the need for the prospect to hire them.

The successful salesperson today practices what I call "modified consultative selling." That is, we selectively consult with prospects on their problems during the initial meeting. We give enough information to convince prospects that we are experts who can help them—but without giving away so much that they can solve the problem themselves and without our help.

For instance, let's say you run a graphic design studio. A prospect asks, "Is there any way to design a brochure that features all six products but could be easily updated if one of the products changes?"

Because you know the answer, your tendency might be to dash off a sketch or fold together a dummy out of scrap paper to show how it's done. Have you sold effectively? No, because the prospect now knows the answer, and can take your solution to his current graphic designer or staff artist or, if the prospect is cheap, directly to a printer.

Instead, you should say, "Yes, that's a requirement we've handled in the past for other customers, and when we're further into the design process, we'll present some options that would work with your particular product." This answer indicates that you are the designer who understands and can solve the problem, but makes it necessary for the prospect to hire you (and not someone else) to get this solution.

And that's the essence of modified consultative selling. Under consultative selling you act like the problem-solving genius at the initial meeting, do everything you can for prospects, and they will hire you out of gratitude and because you're so impressive.

On the other hand, with a *modified* consultative selling approach, you act like the knowledgeable problem solver at the initial meeting, do and say things that convince customers you indeed know the answers, but you don't give the answers away right there. Instead, you disclose just enough information so that customers perceive the need to hire you to get the solution or results they desire.

Be a "sales consultant," by all means, but don't give away the store. Say and do things that demonstrate your abilities and create (rather than eliminate) the need for your services.

ATTRACTION PRINCIPLE #14:

Don't respond instantly to everything that's asked or said the instant the other person says it. Think about it first.

Because you are busy and time pressured, you may be in too much of a hurry to get issues resolved and move on to closing the sale.

There can be a benefit to not responding instantly to everything that's said or happens. For instance, if there's an awkward silence in a negotiation of debate, the first person who talks usually loses.

Kurt, an industrial chemist, smokes a pipe because it gives him an edge in these awkward silences. He fiddles with this pipe, puffing away, while the other person has nothing to occupy his hands. "The other party gives up and invariably speaks first," says Kurt.

I am constantly asked by salespeople for advice on how to respond to the questions, "What do you charge?" or "What does it cost?" The worst mistake you can make is to assume that you have to give an answer on the spot. You don't.

When someone gets to price and asks me "What does it cost?", I respond by first asking them a lot of questions, the purpose of which (I explain) is to gather the information I need to prepare an accurate estimate. After I am done, I say, "I have what I need. Let me go away, work up an estimate, and we will get back to you with it within 24 hours."

Only once did a customer press me for an immediate price quotation, and I buckled under the pressure, blurting out a figure that was way lower than I should have charged. Unfortunately, it was a monthly fee, and I ended up living with it for several years. Fortunately, when the customer was acquired by another company, the new owner canceled the contract, and I was finally freed of my obligation.

Be Ready to Make a Midstream Correction

Why do so many salespeople stumble painfully through sales presentations? Because they haven't planned what they are going to say in advance. Planning means not only having a well-practiced presentation, but also knowing what to say in reply to prospect comments, questions, and objections.

The key to being polished and smooth is to anticipate what prospects will say and prepare, in advance, sensible answers. This way, when prospects say, "But I can get it cheaper from the printer around the corner," instead of saying, "Uhh . . . well . . . ummm," you launch immediately into a confident, clear explanation of why you should print the brochure even though you cost a bit more.

When you are prepared, you feel confident speaking with prospects and customers. When you are not prepared, you are nervous, because you're afraid they'll state an objection or ask a question to which you have no answer. The more prepared you are, the less likely this will occur.

One executive told me, "I am ill at ease meeting potential customers for the first time, because I don't know what to say to get the conversation going." My advice: Visit their websites and check their press releases for recent news. Then use this information as a starting point. For example: "I heard you just got ISO 14000 certification at your Michigan plant. How's that working out for you?"

However, being prepared does not mean being inflexible. Yes, your presentation should be planned. But be willing and able to change course midstream if the prospect takes the conversation in a direction you didn't intend to go.

Recently we had Mike, a general contractor, come to our home to give an estimate on adding a family room. Mike, a creative and talented professional, had his vision of what a family room should be. Unfortunately, it conflicted with the family room I had dreamed of having. Mike insisted that at the rear of the room, there should be sliding glass doors leading onto a deck. I, however, do not like sliding glass doors. I don't like the temptation and easy entry they offer burglars, nor do I like the heat loss in winter.

I explained this to Mike. He countered with an explanation of what a wonderful view the doors would give me. I told him a window would do just as nicely. He countered with an explanation of how a rear door adds value to the home. After going back and forth a few times, it should have been clear to Mike that I didn't want sliding glass doors.

At that point, he should have rearranged his presentation to meet my needs. For instance, he might have suggested a fireplace or a wood-burning stove or wall-to-wall built-in bookcases for the kind of cozy family room I envisioned. But he was inflexible. He wanted to design a family room with sliding glass doors and one of his famous decks, and nothing else would do for me.

After fifteen minutes I became impatient, quickly ended the conversation, and showed Mike the door. It's possible I may still give him the job—I like him and his work—but his sales presentation actually decreased the probability of this happening.

And that's the risk of being inflexible. If you refuse to listen to prospects, to acknowledge their ideas and wishes, and to tailor your presentation to show that you understand and want to meet their needs.

In short, if you insist on doing it your way and your way only—your sales presentation—not only won't get you a go-ahead but may actually make prospects less inclined to hire you. Yes, an ineffective meeting with a prospect can actually unsell you and your services!

PROSPECT REPELLANT #9:

Arguing with the customer or telling him he is wrong.

We've all had this experience: you get several quotes for a product or service. You think about it and then pick one, based on price, style, availability, the personality of the salesperson, the reputation of the company, the warranty, or any of dozens of other reasons—wise or not.

One of the losing bidders calls to follow up. You politely thank him for his bid, tell him you've gone with another source, but (just to lessen the blow) say there may be future opportunity. He asks whom you've chosen, and when you tell him, he says—almost angrily and in a grim tone: "You are making a mistake. They are not as good as us and everyone who goes with them is unhappy."

Even if it's true, what good is saying that? You have already signed a contract. You are already committed. Your only reaction is resentment: The salesperson has just said you made a dumb decision, and by extension is calling you dumb. How does he think that will endear him to you in any way?

Don't tell your customer he's wrong. By disrespecting his opinion, you've set yourself up for a sales disaster. Now you not only stand a good chance of losing the sale—you have to mend your relationship if you hope to do future business.

A generation ago, prospects were much more open to being guided by strong-willed salespeople. Now that consumers are able to do product research on the Internet, they are more empowered with the knowledge they need to make their own decisions. In some instances, they know product facts the salespeople don't, such as that they can get the same item for 10 percent less on a website the sales rep doesn't even know about!

Consumers feel in control. In more and more selling situations, they are in control. When a consumer is a "do it yourself" researcher and shopper, they feel smart that they're such proactive buyers.

Be careful when criticizing or contradicting something customers know, feel, or believe. And do so only if (a) necessary to making the sale, and (b) you are confident in your knowledge and have the facts to back up your claims.

Don't Overpromise

How honest should you be about your abilities and the results you expect to achieve for the prospects? The position I advise you to take is: Present yourself and your products and services in the most favorable light possible without misrepresenting yourself.

Financial services marketing expert Denny LeBarron advises consultants, "Don't make any commitments or claims you can't live up to." I agree. But at the same time, remember that your competitors are puffing their own abilities and making themselves look good. They stretch the truth, exaggerate. Some even just plain lie.

You should not lie, but in the face of all this hype, it doesn't pay to be overly modest either. Management consultant Gary Blake gives this advice: "Present yourself as about 10 percent better than you really are." My feeling is that you shouldn't lie or exaggerate, but you should present yourself as the very best you can be and have been.

As the song says, "Accentuate the positive." Tell all the good things about your service. Highlight your successes. Don't go out of your way to tell prospects about your weaknesses and failures. Your competitors will gladly do that for you. Present yourself in the most favorable light possible while maintaining complete honesty and integrity. Prospects want to hire people who are successful, not mediocre. Position yourself as such.

PROSPECT REPELLANT #10:

Taking on prospects for whom your product is not a good fit.

Have you ever asked someone who was trying to sell you something a question like "Is my job too small for you?" or "Is my account big enough for you to give it your full attention?" You asked these ques-

> tions because you sensed that your account was in fact not a good fit for the seller's business, products, or services.
>
> For example, in a bear market, stock brokers who normally handle customers with minimum portfolios of $1 million will temporarily "lower their standards" and pursue investors with accounts of $500,000 or even, if business is really slow, $100,000.
>
> You know that when the market picks up steam again, those brokers will concentrate on their million-dollar customers, and your small account will likely be neglected. If you have just $100,000 to invest, you are probably better off going to a broker who specializes in customers like you and for whom $100,000 is a good account.

As a seller, you are better served taking on prospects who are a good fit for you. You are likely to under-service or resent accounts with whom you are mismatched, and when your customers pick up on this, they will resent it.

Give the Prospect Choices, but Don't Overwhelm Her with Options

Most of us can handle a limited number of data points when analyzing any decision or purchase. It is much easier for the prospect to make ten "A/B" decisions in sequence (e.g., three or four-bedroom?) than simultaneously deciding on twenty variables when being shown similar items (houses).

"Don't give your customer too many choices," advises direct marketing consultant Joan Harris. "This either confuses her, if she's the decision maker, or slows down the process if lots of people have to see it."

This is an old trick of clothing salespeople that can easily be applied to selling services. The clothes sales clerk knows that if a customer is confronted with rack after rack of ties to choose from, he will become overwhelmed and unable to make a decision.

And so the customer does the easy thing, which is to make no decision and walk away. Instead, the sales clerk begins narrowing the choices: "Do you want silk or polyester?" You say silk. The polyester ties are removed from the counter. "Do you want plain or patterns?" You say patterns.

Solid color ties are removed from the counter. "Stripes or polka dots?" You say stripes. Polka dot ties are taken away. "Do you prefer bright colors or pastels?" This continues until two or three ties remain. Then the close: "Do you want this one, this one, this one, or all three?"

The point is to not overwhelm prospects with lots of choices. Remember, they are looking to you for guidance. If they seem unsure, say, "We could do it this way or this way. Which do you prefer?" By all means, give prospects choices. Prospects resent being told what to do and like to think it was their decision. But in reality, you control the presentation, presenting enough options to enable choice without causing confusion.

PROSPECT REPELLANT #11:

Overwhelming the prospect with options.

Giving the buyer options is another tricky area for sales. Our instinct tells us: the more choices you give the buyer, the better.

The problem is that too many options and choices overwhelm prospects. They can't balance or process all the data, and so they suffer from "analysis paralysis"—with too many decisions to make, they are unable to make any decision, including the decision to buy.

A better approach is to break the buying process down into steps and limit the consumer's decision to just a few options at each step. A real estate agent will not just show homes at random and hope the prospect can make up her mind. She will begin by narrowing the options: split level or colonial? One- or two-family house? Brick or wood frame? Three or four bedrooms? Swimming pool? On the water or inland?

Deal with Prospects on a Personal, Not Just a Business, Level

Like it or not, personal chemistry is a major factor determining whether prospects hire you. It's really quite simple: People hire people whom they like and feel comfortable with. They avoid hiring people whom they dislike, are afraid of, or who make them uncomfortable.

In certain instances, there will be a strong reaction between two personalities that cannot be avoided or controlled. One person will, for a number of reasons, take an instant and overwhelming liking or disliking to another person.

But in most cases, you can create good chemistry—or at least create behavior that allows good chemistry to grow and flourish. For instance, if you have a big ego, be aware that most people don't like braggarts and egomaniacs. No matter how smart, right, or good you are, many people won't hire you because they can't stand the way you behave.

Suzanne Ramos, a manager at American Express, says she occasionally sees consultants who violate what she considers the unwritten rule that "the customer is always right." They talk too much or come across as overconfident, argumentative, even mildly disdainful or arrogant. She is also alert to people who might be difficult to work with. "Life is too short," she says.

In general, people like others who:

- Are friendly.
- Are warm.
- Are courteous.
- Are polite.
- Are on time.
- Are respectful.
- Like them.
- Share their interests.
- Listen to them.
- Show an interest in them.
- Ask them about themselves.
- Treat them well.
- Help them.

"I make a big effort to have prospects comfortable with me," says freelance writer Mary Beth Lareau. "Businesspeople need to be reassured that you are normal and dependable."

In meeting with prospects, you should not come across as superior, nor should you allow them to put you in a subservient position. The encounter should be treated as a meeting of equals. The prospect is an important person with a need to be fulfilled or a problem to be solved.

You are important because you are the expert who can fill that need or solve that problem. You will feel most comfortable with prospects if you establish with them what Robert Ringer, author of *Looking Out for #1*, calls a "value-for-value relationship." That is, for a relationship to work, both parties must exchange value for value. In the selling of services, the customer exchanges money for your time, expertise, labor, and the benefits or results you provide. In such a relationship, there is no superior or subordinate, merely two equals exchanging equal values.

There is no need to feel—because they are the buyers and you are the seller—that customers are the superior, you the inferior. Indeed, they need you as much as you need them. And in some cases, they need you more than you need them, such as when they have problems no one else can solve, and you have more work than you can handle.

But don't rub that in their faces. Establish yourself as their peer, not their subordinate or superior. When this is accomplished, both parties can proceed happily and with dignity intact.

Enthusiasm is also a key ingredient in any sales situation. "Develop the habit of enthusiasm," advises *The Book of Powerful Secrets*. "Enthusiasm works like a magnet—it draws people and success. It's a pleasing personality trait that people like to be part of. It seems to be contagious—the people around you become enthusiastic too and become more cooperative. Enthusiasm sparks initiative and singleness of purpose."

You must be genuinely enthusiastic about your service and about the prospect's proposed project or assignment. If you're indifferent, disdainful, or just plain bored, you are unlikely to get the job. And if you do get it, you'll probably do it poorly.

How do you show enthusiasm? For once, there's no technique for you to learn, because if you are enthusiastic, it will naturally show through in your voice, attitude, manner, and presentation. By the same token, any lack of enthusiasm will also become apparent to the prospect. So to be successful, only provide services, accept projects, and deal with customers that you can be enthusiastic about. Life is too short to do otherwise!

Ten Additional Tips for Making Successful Sales Presentations

From freelance copywriter Judy Brewerton comes this list of ten more helpful ideas on how to present yourself at the initial customer meeting to secure the order:

1. *Silence is golden.* Nervousness or excitement can make you babble. Instead, sit back, ask one or two short questions, look friendly and expectant, and let prospects tell you all about their problems. When you do want to speak, force yourself to speak slowly, and be brief.

2. *Behave as if you already have the job.* Prospects often forget they called you in (or allowed you to visit) to have a look at your sample case or slide show. As a result, you can often sidestep the whole "audition" mode completely. You can start right in with questions about what the prospect needs and go home with an assignment.

3. *Once you have heard their needs, you now know what to tell them about yourself.* Make sure they hear all the bits that will identify you as the person they want. Find low-key ways to work them into the discussion. Don't include your whole work history (especially the unfortunate parts). Use only the things that relate to the prospect's business or problem.

4. *Don't show your samples, resumes, job photos, or brochures unless you're asked.* Remember, you want to be out of the "job applicant" mode and into the "consultant on the job" mode as fast as possible.

5. *Don't tell the prospect your sad stories.* Stress only the positive.

6. *Prospects only want to associate with success.* Make sure you come across as a success. Hiring a difficult or inept supplier will make prospects look bad to their bosses or customers. No matter how successful they look, your prospects all have defeats in their pasts. They're looking to hook up with someone who can improve their track records, not with a war-torn fellow victim.

7. *Remember who you are—the expert source who helps customers.* In-

stead of stating, "I recently did a big job for Pepsi Cola," say, "I recently helped one of my large customers deal with a problem similar to yours." Remember to protect past customers' anonymity if you're speaking of their problems. The fact that you're discreet might impress this prospect too.

8. *Don't be a name dropper.* Name dropping frequently fails to impress prospects. Many prospects are turned off or bored by it. Besides, why run the risk of fondly dropping the name of someone they despise or dislike? Or risk making them fear that you will betray their confidence when they hire you?

9. *Develop ways to end the meeting profitably.* In other words, ask for the order. If this has been an exploratory meeting about a major project, and you feel you haven't yet been able to seize the inside track, try mentioning a smaller part of the project, and ask to do it independently. Say, "Why not let me do that for you right now? Then you'll have that taken care of, and you can see how I work firsthand."

10. *Don't hang around.* You're an enthusiastic, friendly consultant who'd love to do business with them. (Be sure to say so.) But because you're so capable, you're also busy, so don't hang around. Hanging around gives the impression that your time, which you're trying to sell to this prospect for a hefty price, is not valuable.[1]

ATTRACTION PRINCIPLE #15:

Dress for success.

According to Krug's, the men's retailer, a job applicant who does not dress properly for the interview will be turned down 84 percent of the time, and if you do not dress properly at work, you will be passed over for promotion 78 percent of the time.

A study at the University of California found that when people meet, 55 percent of the impression formed is based on appearance, 38 percent on voice quality, and only 7 percent on what is actually said.

In his book, *Business Lunchatations*, successful entrepreneur Bo Dietl explains how appearance goes beyond just being clean and neat, but to fitness and health. Through years of constant exercise, he has built a powerful physique. He radiates health, strength, and energy. "People make instant judgments about you based on a first impression that is formed within the first ten seconds of meeting someone," says Bo. "Physical appearance is responsible for a large portion of this first impression."

As Will Rogers is famous for saying, you never get a second chance to make a first impression. So if you show up at a first meeting with spaghetti sauce on your tie and a five o'clock shadow, that's how your customer or new boss will think of you for years to come.

The rule of thumb: Dress at least as well as the customer, and preferably one step higher.

Note

1. Judy Brewerton, personal communication.

How to Handle "Your Price Is Too High" and Other Common Objections

*There is hardly anything in the world that someone can't make
a little worse and sell a little cheaper, and people who consider
price alone are this man's lawful prey.*

—John Ruskin

Prospects are often repelled when they hear the price, especially if it's high (the term for this is "sticker shock"). In this chapter, we'll look at ways to eliminate price resistance before you quote the actual price, and how to prevent cost from being a barrier to sale. Also covered are ways to overcome other common objections from "We already have a supplier" to "Why should I do business with you?"

Here are some ground rules for handling objections of all kinds:

1. Attitude is everything. Have a positive, friendly, helpful attitude when dealing with objections.

2. Do not convey to prospects that they are stupid or ignorant, that their objections are petty or annoying, or that they are wasting your time.

3. Treat the objection not as a rejection of you but as an uncertainty on the part of the prospect—which it is.

4. Assume this uncertainty is based on lack of data, inaccurate information, or false premises. Your job: to educate prospects so they understand the situation correctly.

5. Never say to prospects, "You're wrong." Few things make people angrier and more defensive than being told they are wrong or stupid.

6. After prospects voice an objection, repeat it back to them in their own words to acknowledge that you heard and understand. For instance, "So you're saying that you prefer a modern design in the living room, even though the rest of the first floor is done in antiques?" Prospects will immediately become much more comfortable when they hear their objections acknowledged and taken seriously.

7. Then say, "That's an interesting point. But have you thought about [give your own point of view]?" Then launch into an explanation of why your point of view makes sense.

8. Keep in mind that the prospect doesn't have to be wrong for you to be right. As Jerry Straus of JMW Consultants says, "Instead of 'either/or' think 'and/also.' Instead of 'Either you are right, Mr. Prospect, or I am right,' say, 'You are right in what you say, Mr. Prospect—and here's what else is also possible.'"

   Too many salespeople spend too much time in the counterproductive activity of trying to show prospects why they are wrong rather than trying to help them find a way to solve their problems using your services.

9. Convince prospects that the advantages of hiring you far outweigh the merits of their objection. You do this not by belittling or minimizing the objection but by shifting attention away from it (which typically deals with some minor aspect or feature of your services prospects don't like) to the end result or benefit prospects are seeking (which your services can deliver better than anyone else's).

   For instance, let's say a prospect says, "I don't like the green computer paper your monthly computer reports are printed on." Assuming your computer system is inflexible and you can't change the paper, you would say, "I understand. But, tell me, Ms. Prospect, what's more important to you—the color of the paper used in the reports, or the information they contain that will help you manage your accounts receivables and billings so much more precisely and effectively?"

When the prospect answers, "The information, of course," you respond by repeating the key reasons why your system provides better information, thus shifting the prospect's attention away from a minor objection (green paper) and focusing it on the central issues of your service and the prospect's requirements, where it should be.

ATTRACTION PRINCIPLE #16:

Deal with objections without insulting the customer.

You cannot agree with everything every prospect and customer says. But understand that whenever you disagree with someone, you risk making yourself less attractive to them.

So, what do you do when the customer says something you believe is wrong—and if uncorrected, will interfere with closing the sale?

After the statement is made, don't disagree with it. But you must say something in response. Say: "I understand." For example:
Prospect: "Your system doesn't work. It didn't test well on our database."
You: "I understand."

Then ask a question to explore the issue further, such as, "Why do you think the system didn't work well with your customer file?"

Focus on finding a solution. The customer sees this as helpful, which deflects the potential adversarial situation that a disagreement can escalate into.

It's my opinion that people, and that includes prospects and customers, have gotten ruder over the last twenty-five years. I don't think people want to be rude; I think the time pressures of modern society cause them to be rude. I call this "haste-based rudeness," and it is a major societal shift in behavior.

When something doesn't go our way, we become impatient, because we are too busy to stop and fix it. We take out our frustration on waiters, repairmen, and other people who serve us, including salespeople.

Understand that when a prospect shows impatience or abruptness, it has nothing to do with you and everything to do with them. People become irritated because, when you are pressed for time, any problem or hitch seems intolerable—not because they don't like you or want to make you squirm.

One thing I have found works well in today's selling environment, whenever talking with a prospect or customer about anything, is to ask before beginning a discussion: "Is now a good time for you? Or should we set a time to talk about this?"

I use a similar technique when making cold calls or follow-up sales calls. Before I begin talking, I ask the prospect this simple question: "Am I catching you at a bad time?" If they say yes, I ask when would be a better time to talk, and call back at the time and date they select. If they say "no," it's my understanding—and, I believe, theirs too—that they have given me permission to proceed, provided I am relevant, concise, and do not waste their time.

Salespeople are taught in training sessions always to close now, and not later—but in the twenty-first century, this doesn't work any more. People do things according to their own schedule, and when you show respect for their time, you become more attractive to them.

Overcoming Price Objections

To avoid "sticker shock" when quoting a price on an expensive product, quote the price in more palatable terms. If your price sounds too high, rephrase so it sounds less costly.

Instead of $60, offer three easy monthly payments of $19.95 each. Instead of $100, sell it for $99.95. Instead of $22, make it $19 plus $3 shipping and handling. Instead of $1,000, make it $500 upon order and $500 upon delivery.

Look at the collectible ads in the Sunday magazine. Very few people would agree to buy a civil war chess set for hundreds of dollars. So the manufacturer sells it to you one piece at a time. While paying $560 for a chess set seems outrageous and would turn customers off, most of us can handle $17.50 for a "hand-painted solid brass knight, modeled after the civil war cavalry officer."

The best way to handle price resistance is to prevent it from happening in the first place, or at least minimize it. You are more likely to make the sale when your price quotation is within the prospect's budget.

Your best chance of having that happen is to know the budget before you give your price. The best way of knowing the budget before you give your price is simply to ask the prospect what the budget is.

In the movie *Tin Men* starring Richard Dreyfus and Danny DeVito, an aluminum siding salesman goes into a car dealership to buy a new Cadillac. "How much is it?" he asks the car salesman about the car he wants to buy.

"How much do you want to pay?" the car salesman asks. Disgusted by what is an obvious sales tactic, he replies sarcastically, "A dollar . . . I want to pay a dollar."

Many of us don't ask prospects how much they want to pay because we feel that it is somehow sleazy, and that doing so will create an uncomfortable situation.

But if you indeed did know how much your buyers wanted to spend, your sales closing ratio would shoot through the roof—because you'd be quoting prices you knew they could afford and were willing and prepared to spend.

How do you ascertain what the buyer wants to spend without the awkwardness of asking outright?

When it's time to discuss price, ask the buyer, "Do you have a budget?" Note that you are not asking, "What is your budget?" You are instead asking the much less threatening question, "Do you have a budget?"

The buyer can only give one of two answers: yes or no, with about half of prospects saying yes and the other half saying no. If the buyer says "yes," then you ask: "Would you mind sharing with me what your budget is?"

Those prospects who tell you their budget have just given you the range under which your price quotation must fall to be accepted.

But what if the buyer says, "No, we don't have a budget." Then you ask: "Well, do you have a dollar figure in mind of what you would like it to cost?"

Even if they do not have a budget worked out, many people, when asked the question in this way, will come back at you with an answer something like "I was figuring to spend around $1,000 and not more than $3,000."

In effect, they really do have a budget—$1,000 to $3,000—but just never wrote it down or said it out loud before.

A few people, however, will not share their budget no matter how you ask. "I don't want to give you my budget," they will say. "I want YOU to tell ME what it will cost."

In such cases, use the "good, better, best" method of price quotation to increase the odds that you will quote a price acceptable to the buyer. For instance, let's say you are quoting on selling the prospect a half-acre lot with a custom-built home.

Instead of just quoting your top-end home, which is $500,000, you give the prospect three options to choose from.

The first option, which you call GOOD, is a basic three-bedroom home with a fireplace and unfinished basement. It is $300,000—the cheapest you can offer while still giving the buyer a decent home and yourself a decent profit.

The second option, which you call BETTER, is the same home, but with a finished basement and an added sitting room in the master bedroom suite. It is $400,000—your middle-of-the-road model.

The third option, which you call BEST, is the same home as in the BETTER option but with top-of-the-line landscaping, a second fireplace, and a fourth bedroom. It is $500,000—your top-of-the-line model.

You outline all options for the prospect, including the prices. Then instead of asking him whether he wants a home, you ask him, "*Which* do you want—good, better, or best?"

This strategy increases the chances that your price quotation will fall within the dollar amount the prospect wants to pay.

Also, very few people want the lowest-quality of three choices. So some buyers who were looking to pay $300,000 will find a way to pay $400,000 (even if it means a bigger mortgage or borrowing from Uncle Joe)—and more will select BETTER over GOOD.

Here are a few other strategies for handling price-sensitive prospects:

1. Charge a midrange price but offer premium service.

2. Differentiate your product from the competition.

3. Give the prospect a ballpark idea of the price range early in the selling cycle.

4. Find out the budget and quote a solution that fits within that dollar amount.

5. Offer lower-cost alternatives.

6. Offer leasing or other financing options.

7. Express price in the smallest possible increment— e.g., "$1 a day," not "$365 a year."

8. If your price is higher than the competition, focus on justifying the difference, not your total price.

9. Make it easy to buy.

10. Eliminate the risk with a strong guarantee.

Be persistent. Even when consumers aren't of a mind to spend, they still have needs that only money can meet. Therefore, they need to be prodded, reminded, and contacted with much more intensity and frequency to overcome reluctance and inertia. Don't make the mistake of giving up too early when pursuing a qualified prospect. Often it takes five or six calls before they break down and agree to see you, listen to your presentation, or buy your service.

Stress the low cost of acquiring your product or service. Price-conscious customers tend to spend smaller sums, so you should make your service or product appear as inexpensive as possible. For example, if you offer a payment plan, the price should be expressed as a low monthly payment rather than a lump sum: $239.95 a month, not $3,500.

Sell the service or product that's most cost-effective for the prospect, not the one that's most profitable for you. Price-watchers want their vendors to advise them on how to get maximum results at minimal cost. This means you should sell the product or service that best meets their needs, even if it doesn't give you a big profit right now. You should be seeking to make customers, not sales. Build the long-term relationship by doing right by the customer. It will pay off handsomely.

"I Can Get It Cheaper Somewhere Else"

This is similar to "Your price is too high," but with a difference. Here prospects are not telling you they can't afford you or that you are not worth your fee. They're simply noting that your competitor across the street sells a (they think) similar service for less, and why should they pay you $1,000 when they can get the same thing from Company X for only $800?

Why is this objection so popular? Because in reality, it's difficult for prospects to compare your service with your competitors on a feature-by-feature basis.

There are so many variables, so many complexities, and so many uncertainties (after all, services are intangibles) that buyers tend to focus only on the most obvious point of comparison—the price—when deciding between service A and service B. They become confused by a myriad of features and claims, and in disgust mentally give up and say, "Okay, which will cost me less?"

The key to overcoming the objection "I can get it cheaper somewhere else" is to make clear to buyers that they are not comparing apples and apples but rather apples versus oranges. That is, your services are not identical to those of your competitors—you offer many important advantages in terms of quality, credentials, service, reliability, trust-worthiness, experience, and reputation—and so a strict comparison of their price versus yours is not a meaningful exercise. Further, you must convince prospects that the advantages you offer provide extra benefits that far outweigh the extra price you're asking.

It's basic to human nature: We all want to get the best and pay the least. Unfortunately, the laws of supply and demand say that excellence costs. And deep down we know that the best product or service is rarely the one with the lowest price.

So remind prospects of this. They want the best, so the fact that they can get it cheaper elsewhere is really beside the point, isn't it? Remind them, in your own words, of what English critic John Ruskin said about price-shopping (see chapter opening quote). One way to do this without being offensive is to help prospects recall a time when they bought on price only and were later sorry they did:

Prospect: "I am talking to someone locally who can do the job for a lot less money."

You: "I understand. But let me ask: Have you ever in the past chosen someone because his price was the lowest, only to be disappointed once the job was done?"

Another effective technique is to ask prospects point-blank if they are price shoppers (some people are).

Prospect: "I am talking to someone locally who can do the job for a lot less money."

You: "Let me ask . . . are you primarily concerned with price—or with [reliability, service, quality, or whatever advantage you offer]?"

Most prospects will insist that they want quality, service, or some other advantage you offer. You must then offer proof that you can deliver these benefits and get prospects to agree that superior quality and service quite naturally cost a bit more (but the results are worth it).

A few prospects will tell you, "I buy primarily on price" or "It's a competitive bid situation." Unless you feel certain your price will be the lowest, don't bother pursuing such prospects.

Say, "I understand. Some people prefer to buy primarily on price, and my service is not for them. But do call me when you have a job that needs my special touch and you have a budget that will allow us to work together. I'm looking forward to it!"

Point out to prospects that it's cheaper to hire you now and get the job done right than to hire an inferior service, pay the fee, then pay you again to correct their mistakes:

Prospect: "I am talking to someone locally who can do the job for a lot less money."

You: "As a licensed contractor, I spend a lot of time getting paid to correct the work of local handymen who do not have the expertise or training to do this type of work correctly. Surely it would be less expensive to have the job done right the first time, rather than pay for an inferior job performed by an unqualified source now, then pay me to fix it later on . . . do you agree?"

Compare your credentials, track record, results achieved for customers, and other qualifications with the competing firms. If you have a strong record of proven success and a long list of satisfied customers, stress these. Customers will pay extra if they have more confidence in your ability to get the job done reliably and on time.

Overcoming Stalls

One of the most dreaded customer objections is the stall: "I have to think it over." Here are some responses that can help get past it:

- "What exactly do you want to think about?"
- "Let's think it over out loud. Sometimes two heads are better than one."
- "Let's think it over while it is fresh in your mind. What are some of the items you need to know more about?"

What's the best way to handle stalls and objections? "Give them back to your prospects and work them out together," advises sales expert Brian Azar.

For example, say your prospect wants 24-hour delivery. But the best you can do is 48 hours. Tell the prospect, "If you want it in 24 hours, we've got a problem, since we can only get it to you in 48 hours." Then ask, "What can we do to resolve this?"

If your prospect doesn't offer any legitimate solution, ask, "Is there another company that can offer you 24-hour service?"

If the prospect answers "yes," ask: "Why aren't you using them? What are you hoping that we can do that they can't?" Then address the issue that emerges.

Most of the time, however, when you ask, "Is there another company that can take care of this?" the prospect will answer "no." Other companies can't do better—or they say they can, but don't deliver on the promise.

Find out whether the objection is really important. If you truly can't solve it, disqualify the prospect before you spend time making a presentation.

ATTRACTION PRINCIPLE #17:

Sometimes another product or service is a better match for the prospect's needs than yours is. When you tell prospects this, you may lose a sale today, but you win a fan for life, and eventually, you'll get their orders.

When this happens, let the other vendor take the job. Don't fight for business you really aren't qualified to handle. Instead, concentrate on finding situations where your offer is a better fit than the competition's.

The idea is to show the customer that you have her best interests at heart by actually having her best interests at heart. When you tell a prospect, "Buy from my competitor; they are better qualified to help you here than we are," the prospect will be amazed and grateful. And she will want to show her gratitude both by giving you some of her business and referring others to you.

If you don't have better price, quality, or service than the competition, here's the one thing you can say that will absolutely dazzle the customer: "This isn't an area of strength for us. Why don't you call

XYZ Company?" Then suggest someone in your network who is better qualified. Your reputation will soar, and the return referrals from your networking connection will more than make up for the business you turned away.

In the movie *Miracle on 34th Street*, Kris Kringle—a man who claims he is the real Santa Claus, and in fact may be—gets a job as a department store Santa Claus at Macy's in New York City around Christmas time. When a customer asks about a gift item she wants to buy, Kringle tells her, "We don't have it; try Gimbel's across the street."

At first the store manager who hired Kringle is infuriated that his Santa Claus sent a customer to their fiercest competitor, and is going to fire him. But then the customer tells the store manager, "I was so impressed that your store helped me even though there was no sale in it for you, I shall do all of my shopping here from now on."

The store manager realizes that helping customers, even if it means a loss in the short term, is a great tool for the long term, and makes it standard store policy, telling all clerks: "If we don't have what the customer wants, tell them where they can get it."

Embarrassment

Another objection, often unvoiced, is that the prospect is somehow embarrassed to buy or own your product or service. For instance, an adult man who is a metrosexual may indulge himself in manicures, but if he is a construction worker, he might not want his coworkers to know about this.

Advertising legend Alvin Eicoff tells the story of how a radio commercial he created to sell rat poison to farmers failed to generate orders. Puzzled, he went on the road to ask farmers why they didn't buy.

"I don't want my neighbors to know I have rats in the barn," a farmer told Eicoff, "and they'd find out when they saw the package being delivered by the mail carrier."

Eicoff added a line to the radio commercials about the poison being delivered in a plain brown wrapper. Sales soared.

"What's the Catch?"

Has this happened to you? You're in the process of selling your widgets to a prospect. You've turned features into benefits. You've given him an amazing demonstration. You've attempted several closing techniques.

Overall, you've done such a marvelous job of proving the value of your widget, that you're convinced he's ready to sign on the dotted line. Suddenly, he hits you with: "What's the catch?"

Most people have been taught to believe that if it sounds too good to be true, it probably is. Sometimes, you can oversell to the point where your prospect thinks there has to be a catch.

Your response to this question can be critical. If you say, "There's NO catch," your prospect will, nevertheless, assume you must be hiding something. So what is the best way to handle this situation?

First, be prepared for it. Don't get caught with your pants down. Hesitation or stunned silence will lose you the sale every time.

You may even want to provoke the subject before your customer does with the question, "You're probably wondering what the catch is, right?" Then, give your customer a catch that is true yet meaningless to him.

"Years ago, I worked for a promotional company that sold coupon books to golfers by phone," says sales consultant Randy Ruggles.[1] "The golfer who purchased a book would receive six rounds of golf for the price of one. The deal definitely sounded too good to be true."

Ruggles's closing technique went something like this:

RR: "Now, I bet you're wondering what the catch is, right Bob?"

Bob: (Laughs) "Yes, I am."

RR: "Well, you're right. There is one catch."

Bob: "I knew it." (Bob tenses, preparing for the worst.)

RR: "The catch is that the golf course owner requests that you call in advance to book your tee-off time. But you probably do that anyway, don't you?"

Bob: "Usually I do, yeah. That's it?"

RR: "That's it, Bob."

Bob: "Sounds great."

RR: "Great! So how many books would you like, one or two?"

See how Randy gave Bob a catch to earn his trust—but made it a catch he can live with?

Try this technique yourself the next time you're faced with the "too good to be true" scenario: Find a small catch about your product; create one if you have to. Just make sure it's a catch that your prospect doesn't care about. You'll gain credibility in his eyes and close a lot more sales in the long run.

Not Ready to Buy

Another common objection is timing: the prospect says he is not ready to make a decision or buy.

Top sales trainer Bill Caskey suggests the following script for handling this situation[2]:

Prospect: "You know, I'm not really sure we want to buy this at this time. We have a lot of other things going on and we just don't have the time to devote to it."

You: "I totally understand. Maybe this isn't the right time. The last thing I want to do is create more problems for you. You told me last month that you had some severe problems you were trying to solve, but now it sounds like those have disappeared." (NOTE: You know they haven't, but you must always go back to the original "compelling reason" why they need what you are selling.)

Prospect: No, they really haven't gone away. I just don't know if this is the time to solve them.

You: I don't either. Sounds like that leaves us a couple of choices. One, we can stop and forget we even started this. I can go on to my next project and you can continue dealing with the problem. Or, we can start over and figure out if this problem is really something you want to fix. I must tell you that I'm OK with either outcome.

Prospect: No. the problem still hasn't been fixed. And it still is a serious problem. So, I suppose we should continue.

PROSPECT REPELLANT #12:

Discouraging the prospect from "thinking about it."

There are more smarmy comebacks in Sales Training 101 for when the prospect says, "I want to think about it" than for virtually any other objection. One that is particularly offensive is, "Why do you want to think about it?" . . . the obvious answer from the prospect being, "So I make the right decision."

When the prospect says, "I want to think about it," your response should be as follows:

"I understand. You want to make sure you're making the right decision. Usually when a prospect tells me he wants to think about it, it means he has a question about the product I haven't answered or needs additional information before he can make a purchase decision. What question do you have that I haven't answered about this product, or what missing piece of information do you need before you can make a buying decision?"

When you ask this, most prospects will respond by asking you the question or telling you what else they need to know. These give you the specific objections in their minds you must overcome to close the sale.

How to "Read the Prospect's Mind"

You cannot overcome an objection unless you are aware of it. But many times, the prospects keep their objections to themselves. They do not share the objection with the salesperson; they just keep saying "no" or not buying.

So it's important to get the prospect to tell you her objections so they are out in the open. But how?

Here's a technique that may work for you: After making your sales presentation, pause, and ask the prospect: "How does that sound—good, bad, or terrible?"

If the prospect answers "good," you can proceed to the next step in the sales cycle. If the prospect answers "bad" or "terrible," ask her what she doesn't like. Then address these concerns so you can move the sale forward.

Notes

1. Randy Ruggles, *Sales Tip of the Month* (2004).
2. Bill Caskey, *Same Game, New Rules* (Indianapolis: Winpointe Publishing, 2003), p. 128.

Magnetic Closings

In the movie *Out of Sight*, George Clooney is a charming thief who, while serving a prison term, tells fellow prisoner Albert Brooks, "You'd be surprised at all you can get if you ask for things in the right way."

Closing is asking for an order . . . in the right way. By asking for the order in the "right way," you can increase the intensity of the customer's commitment and attraction to you at closing time so you close more and bigger sales, more often—and avoid the common mistakes salespeople make that foul the deal at this critical juncture.

"Closing" means getting the order. For product sellers, this means getting a signed contract or purchase order. For service sellers, it means getting the prospect to agree to retain you, or at least make a tentative commitment contingent upon final approval of your fee and contract.

Many businesspeople understandably don't enjoy pressuring prospects and would prefer that potential customers close themselves by saying, "Okay, let's go, I'm ready to buy." Others, many of whom work on Wall Street, enjoy closing and pushing for the order.

Unfortunately, fewer and fewer prospects close themselves these days. Consumers are more hesitant to spend money and more likely to examine each purchasing decision more carefully than they did ten years ago. As a result, you are going to have to bring up and negotiate the final details of the deal if you want to get the order.

Closing is necessary because it overcomes prospect resistance, inertia, and ignorance. Prospects are resistant because, like most people, they hate to part with money. They suffer from inertia—the natural tendency of all objects, animate and inanimate, to resist action and movement.

Worse, they are also, to a degree, ignorant, because even if they want to hire you, they're not quite sure how to go about it. Do they sign a contract? Write you a letter? Phone? Pay some money up front? Try your system for thirty days? Lease, rent, or buy your equipment?

When people are unsure of what to do next, their choice is to do nothing. By closing, you provide prospects with welcome guidance on what the next step is and how to take it. So if you want the prospect's business, you've got to step forward and ask for it—clearly, forcefully, directly, and persuasively.

Seven Keys to Closing the Sale

Ever notice how some people seem to be able to sell anything to anybody? It's not that they're born salespeople. Successful salespeople have studied sales techniques and they know how to apply them. Successful selling is a science as much as an art. This means, if you use your head and try to understand your customer, you can take control of the situation and get the results you want.

Here are seven keys that can help you get the customer to say "yes" at the most critical point in the sale—the closing:

1. *Overcome objections.* Objections are those reasons your prospects or customers give for not wanting to buy. Sometimes they give you their objections voluntarily; often you have to dig for them. An inexperienced salesperson will want to gloss over these "negatives" and ignore them. An effective

salesperson knows that objections are real barriers that must be confronted head on and surmounted.

Get the person to give you specific objections. You may hear the response, "This isn't a good time for me to buy." Ask, "Why not?" and most of the time you'll hear the person say, "I want to think it over." Then ask, "What do you need to think about?" Maybe the person had doubts about your product that you can now clear up. Maybe you haven't spelled out the benefits in a convincing, compelling fashion yet.

2. *Offer reasons to buy now.* Prepare some solid reasons as to why the person will benefit from buying now, not later. Perhaps the price is going up or the product will not be available. Don't use these ploys unless you can be absolutely truthful doing so.

Perhaps your customer is missing out on health benefits or dollars-and-cents savings by procrastinating. Spell out what those losses are: "You're losing $5 a week until you buy this product," or, "You're endangering your health until you start filtering your drinking water."

3. *Help the person solve problems.* Have the vital information handy. Will the item fit in his work space? Have the dimensions at hand. Memorize the facts or have a "data sheet" handy.

Often people see things they want but the problem is being able to afford them. Solve this by offering different payment plans. Perhaps one customer would be happier making a deposit and paying the balance on delivery. Another person might be more comfortable making monthly installments. Still another prefers paying up front for the stripped-down model without the "bells and whistles." Be sympathetic to the person's financial dilemma, listen carefully and offer a solution that fits the individual situation.

4. *Narrow the choices.* Some customers get confused when they see too many different options. They like this color and that pattern. The more they see, the more complex the decision becomes for them.

Your job is to start eliminating items. Get rid of choices that are too expensive. Then eliminate those that are inappropriate for other reasons. When the customer says, "Don't throw out that one," you need to ask, "What do you like about it?"

Once you know exactly what your customer is looking for, usually you can pull it out of your sample case or go right to it in your catalog. Often enough a person who was just making excuses will decide to buy when confronted with the very thing he said he was looking for.

Sometimes a prospect will let you know an item is not quite right. Maybe the person would prefer another color or another style. Then ask, "If I can get it for you in black, will you buy it?"

5. *Help the person reach a decision.* No one wants to be seen as indecisive. When you sense that someone has made a selection but not a decision, point out why this is a good choice. As you go back over the benefits, personalize them, making them fit with what you've learned about your customer's needs. Just don't pressure the person.

6. *Ask for the sale.* An inexperienced salesperson will wait for the customer to say, "I'll take it." This doesn't always happen. In fact, some customers want to be asked. "May I go ahead and reserve one of these for you? Are you ready to sign up?" The way you ask depends on what you're selling, but don't be afraid to ask the customer point blank to make the decision to buy.

7. *Take "no" for an answer.* When your customer says "no," and means it, don't let any disappointment show. Some salespeople go from hot to cold at the sound of "no," leaving the customer to think: all that politeness was just sales technique! Wish the person a good day and keep smiling until you're out the door . . . you just may have a sale the next time you call.

ATTRACTION PRINCIPLE #18:

No prospect is indispensable. Another will always come to take his or her place. You become magnetically attractive to prospects by understanding this and not giving off a vibe that makes you seem needy and desperate.

Approximately 675,642 people are born every hour. So don't worry if you lose a prospect. There will be 675,642 new ones within an hour to take his place.

> Is your market small businesses? There are more than 10 million small businesses in the United States. So if one doesn't buy from you, there is no shortage of other opportunities to make sales in the small business marketplace.

Salespeople get particularly anxious when courting a potential national account. Yet even national accounts are not irreplaceable. If you are pursuing a business opportunity with a Fortune 500 customer, and you lose the competition, there are 499 other Fortune 500 companies to call on. Even better, that same Fortune 500 company has many other divisions that operate somewhat autonomously, and may hire you even when others do not.

Closing One Step at a Time

In sales lingo, closes can be categorized as "major" or "minor." A major close is prospects saying "Yes, we'll take it." Before that occurs, there will typically be a series of minor or incremental closes. These "incremental closes" involve getting prospects to agree to different ideas, concepts, and suggestions you propose as you talk your way to the close of the sale.

Basically, this technique involves getting prospects to say yes to a number of mini-proposals you present orally. Each mini-proposal covers one of the items or conditions of the sale. Taken together, they are the total package of services you want to sell the prospect. For example, an ad agency producing a catalog for a customer has to quote on several aspects—photography, illustration, design, copy, printing.

After getting prospects to say yes to each mini-proposal, you then sum up the total package, noting that they have agreed to each point. Finally, you restate your proposition in its entirety and get prospects to finalize the agreement.

First, I get customers to agree to each point concerning the deal we are making. Once they've done that, how can they say no to my final proposition, as it merely sums up a number of points they've already said yes to?

For instance, here's how I used this technique recently with a prospect who wanted me to write a mailing piece promoting his graphic design studio.

> **Me**: "So Mr. Green, I understand you are looking for a direct mail piece to generate sales leads that will result in new customers for your design studio."
>
> **Prospect**: "Yes."
>
> **Me**: "As we've discussed, the best format would be a sales letter with an illustrated brochure and reply card."
>
> **Prospect**: "Yes."
>
> **Me**: "And you would prefer that it be mailed in a personally addressed, standard-size business envelope."
>
> **Prospect**: "Yes, that's correct."
>
> **Me**: "We've gone over my fee schedule and you understand that it's $1,200 to write the brochure, $950 for a one-page letter, and $150 for the reply card."
>
> **Prospect**: "Fine. I have no problem with that."
>
> **Me**: "And you would like to have a first draft of the copy in two weeks or sooner, is that right?"
>
> **Prospect**: "Yes."
>
> **Me**: "And because you're a design firm, you'll handle all the graphics and design of the piece yourself."
>
> **Prospect**: "Yes."
>
> **Me**: "Okay. So let me prepare an agreement that spells all that out for you: I'll be writing a lead-generating direct mail package, with letter, brochure, and reply card, that is due two weeks from today, for a fee of $2,300 total."
>
> **Prospect**: "Fine."

See the technique? First I get customers to agree to each point concerning the deal we are making. Once they've done that, how can they say no to my final proposition, as it merely sums up a number of points they've already said yes to?

A series of small or incremental closes, in which you get prospects to say "yes" to each step of the deal, makes it easy to go for the final close, where it is almost impossible for prospects to refuse you.

Of course, if prospects say "no" to one of your intermediate closes, then it becomes an objection, and you either must overcome that objection or remove that particular element from the agreement you are trying to finalize.

Close Like a Pro

The professional salesperson doesn't tell the customer. He asks questions, finds out what the customer wants, then provides an opportunity for the customer to make a choice.

Most people like to be seen as decision makers. Early in your presentation or even before making the appointment, ask "Will you need to consult anyone else before placing the order?" If someone says, "Well, I really should consult my spouse," you can say, "I'll bet your spouse trusts your judgment to take advantage of a good deal when you see it." You can even say, "I'll bet your boss trusts your judgment enough."

Yet many people have difficulty making decisions, especially in purchasing something for themselves, like clothing or jewelry, or something for the home. You've probably seen sales lost because the customer couldn't decide between several items or several colors and ends up being too confused to purchase anything. You can overcome indecision by asking the customer to make choices at every step of your presentation.

Suppose you're selling jewelry items. Bring out two, to start, then ask your customer which she prefers. When she tells you, put the other one away, then bring out a third and ask her to choose again. After three or four choices, your customer is looking at something she herself has chosen over other alternatives. Very likely, she'll buy.

If you're only offering a couple of items, you could bring the customer to make a choice this way. "This is a nice sofa, isn't it?" The customer may say, "Yes, it's lovely." Then ask, "Do you like it as well as the first one?" The customer may say, "No," which is your cue to say, "Then the other one is the one you want, isn't it?"

If you're selling something that doesn't require making a selection, give the customer other choices to make. Some questions are: "If we can work out the terms of delivery and payment, can we put in the order today?"

"Would you prefer to take this model or should I order a new one from the factory for you?" "Would you like to write a check for the entire amount or would you like to take advantage of our easy financing plan?" "Would you like to make a deposit of half the amount now and the rest on delivery?"

Sometimes the customer hesitates because he feels that the purchase will be a strain on the budget. When you hear this type of objection, offer empathy. Chances are, you know what it's like to want something that seems too costly.

Chances are, too, you've made some purchases that seemed extravagant at the time, but that you've never had reason to regret. You probably still have those purchases: the good wool suit that never goes out of style, the stainless steel cookware made to last a lifetime, the handmade rug that looks better with age.

Or perhaps it was the little luxury that really lifted your spirits up during a tough time. Tell your customer how you spent "too much," adding, "Some sacrifices are worth it, don't you think?" The customer may decide that this time the expenditure is justified.

Sometimes when the customer seems to be deciding not to buy for lack of money, you can turn this into a reason for buying. People without much money can't afford to be without things that protect the assets they have.

Items such as insurance of various kinds—burglar alarm systems, safes, and smoke detectors—are examples of these items. Again, it's important to empathize with your customer's situation. "I know how it is to be faced with a lot of bills, but what if you were faced with replacing your home? I don't think you'll ever regret deciding to take advantage of this offer."

Suppose the item you're selling costs $240 and your customers says, "That's a lot of money!" Instead of disagreeing, empathize. "Yes $240 at one time is a lot of money." Then go on to show that if the item lasts three years, it only costs $80 a year.

Give your customer a chance to think about this. Then add, "Now, we could break that $240 down into payments of just $20 per month for a year or $10 a month for two years." When a sum that seemed high becomes affordable, you're likely to have a sale.

It's always the customer, not the salesperson, who decides. Show you understand where your customer is coming from and ask questions that will lead your customer to the choice you're hoping for.

When you give the price, be clear about whether you are giving the customer a quote or an estimate. What's the difference? According to an article in the newsletter *Overcoming Objections*, a quote implies a fixed amount that the customer expects not be exceeded. An estimate refers to an educated guess that customers know may vary as work commences.

Use an Inexpensive "Deal Sweetener"

To close a difficult sale, offer a special inducement. This offer of a "deal sweetener"—something extra for free—might very well be responsible for your getting the order.

Deal sweeteners take many forms. Yours might be a reduction in price; an easy credit feature like "no money down"; a special trade-in allowance; a discount for cash; a bonus for quantity buying; merchandising or advertising support. Remember when your mother took you across town so you could get that free Scout knife with your new suit? That was an extra inducement.

The reason deal sweeteners don't close more sales is because so many salesmen reveal them too early. The extra inducement is not a "thermometer" to take the prospect's temperature and judge how ready he is to deal; it's a clincher, a closer. If you use yours to find out whether or not the prospect is hot, you're making it part of the purchase, and robbing it of its dramatic appeal.

If you can make your sale without using your deal sweetener, give your customer the benefit of it after he signs the order—as a bonus. Such a gesture will make him feel even more pleased with his decision, and will cause him to talk you up to his friends, neighbors, and colleagues.

How to Close When Selling to Committees

When you are selling to a committee, make sure all the decision makers—all of them—will be in the room when you are ready to close. If all decision makers are not present, the prospect can avoid signing at any time with the simple excuse, "So-and-so is not here and we need his approval" . . . and there is absolutely no way to overcome this stall. The only way to overcome it is to avoid it in the first place, by insisting that every decision maker be present for this particular meeting.

Even then, selling to a committee can have its problems! In his book *Confessions of an Advertising Man*, David Ogilvy, founder of the ad agency Ogilvy & Mather, relates his experience in selling his agency's services to a committee:

> Some years ago, we were invited to compete for an association account. I duly presented myself at their headquarters and was ushered into a pompous committee room.
>
> "Mr. Ogilvy," said the chairman, "we are interviewing several agencies. You have exactly fifteen minutes to plead your case. Then I will ring this bell, and the representative of the next agency, who is already waiting outside, will follow you."
>
> Before launching into my pitch, I asked three questions:
>
> "How many of the end user markets must be covered in your campaign?" Answer: automobile tires, furnishing fabrics, industrial products, women's clothing, men's clothing.
>
> "How much money is available?" Answer: $600,000.
>
> "How many people must OK the advertisements?" Answer: the twelve members of the committee representing twelve manufacturers.
>
> "Ring the bell!" I said, and walked out.[1]

Asking the right questions will help you accurately assess the client's requirements.

How to Accurately Assess the Prospect's Requirements

You will have gathered a lot of preliminary information in your meeting with the customer by asking the right questions, as discussed in Chapter 3.

Ask whatever additional questions will help you make an estimate of the scope of the project, time frame, work involved, and your fee. If the prospect has done similar projects in the past, ask what the budgets were for those projects. A winning bid for the current project will probably be somewhere in that range.

If most of your projects require prospects to answer basically the same set of questions you've asked previous customers, consider creating a questionnaire the prospects can fill out and return to you. If the selling process stalls because you and the prospect aren't sure what should happen next, you can say that the next step is to complete and mail the form. Another way to move forward is to ask the prospect, "What do you want to happen next?" then do what is asked of you.

Do You Need to Write a Formal Proposal?

It depends. If the prospect issues an official Request for Proposal (RFP), it's probably necessary to answer with a formal proposal if you want to win the contract.

The leading authority on proposals is the late author Herman Holtz, and his book, *Proven Proposal Strategies to Win More Business* (Dearborn, 1997), is in my view the authoritative guide to the topic of proposal writing for consultants.

If a prospect doesn't ask for a formal proposal, don't write one. Proposals are time consuming. "Proposals should not be a sailing expedition to see if the prospect will agree with a course," writes consultant Alan Weiss. "Send a proposal as a confirmation, not an exploration."

Not doing proposals is actually a sales strategy used by some service providers who position themselves as busy and in demand. The rationale being that writing a proposal gives away a lot of my time and information for free, which is something I don't do, because there is a large and continual demand for my services.

Some potential customers have told me, "There are other firms we are interviewing, and they are willing to write a proposal and give us ideas for free." My reply is, "If they have time to give away their advice and expertise for free, how good could they be? The advice is probably worth what you are paying for it: nothing."

If the customer needs some sort of written summary of the work scope and your cost estimate, use a short letter of agreement, even a memo, rather than a formal proposal. I don't like the term proposal, since it positions me as someone hoping to get business. If I send a letter or memo serving as a proposal, I label it "Preliminary Recommendations." This implies that (a) the customer is getting useful advice, not a sales pitch and (b) the advice is preliminary, and the real solution will be provided only when I am retained.

If I am presenting a price to a customer, I usually label the document as a "cost estimate" rather than a quotation or bid. An article in the newsletter *Overcoming Objections* states that a quote implies a fixed amount that the customer expects you not to exceed. An estimate, by comparison, refers to an educated guess that customers know may vary as work commences.

On the other hand, many businesses close lots of big contracts with proposals. But it has to be clear and easy to follow. "In a competitive situation, a great proposal can provide an advantage only if the information is pertinent and understood by the client," writes Adam Erlich.

More Tips for Closing the Sale

Keep in mind that not every prospect will agree to your terms, fees, and conditions. When they say "no," it usually has nothing to do with you—and everything to do with their budgets, needs, personalities, and priorities.

Some people will not budge, even when rational proposals and accommodating compromises are presented by the seller. It's not worth your time trying to convince them to see things more clearly.

"It is generally futile to argue with people who are dogmatic in their beliefs," wrote Sydney Harris in *Soap Box Journal*. "They have a deep emotional investment in defending their prior positions, and the more you try to pry them loose, the more stubbornly they think."

Closing requires that you come right out and say to the prospect, "I would like to have you as a customer. May we get started?" This makes many professionals uncomfortable. Many of us were taught that asking for the order is inappropriate. It is not.

Consultant Ilise Benun has developed a wonderful line that can be used both during intermediate stages of the sales cycle as well as at closing. It's effective in moving the prospect one step closer to a final decision in a way that is not adversarial and does not make you seem desperate or overeager for the order.

When you reach a point where it seems you should move forward, but the prospect doesn't seem to know what to do next and doesn't suggest a course of action, say to the prospect, "What do you want to happen next?" This works beautifully because the prospect tells you what is required to consummate the transaction.

The more time and effort prospects invest in making the decision whether to buy from you, the more likely you are to close the sale. This doesn't mean you should waste prospects' time or make it deliberately difficult for them to communicate with you. Far from it.

But it does mean that if you can get prospects to invest their time and effort in a relationship with you before you are officially retained to perform services on a paid basis, you are more likely to get the assignment than someone with whom prospects have not invested a lot of time and effort.

"If a customer asks you to sit in on a developmental meeting, whether you are paid for that effort are not, you are the vendor of choice," says business writer Paul D. Davis. "I have never, except once, had a customer give an assignment to someone else after I helped with the concept and planning of that project."

Consider this scenario. You have been talking with a prospect on and off for the past six months. She's visited your office two or three times, and you've exchanged lots of letters and information.

Now she's ready to hire a consultant to handle her firm's outplacement. Who will she be more likely to hire? You, a person with whom she is already familiar and comfortable, or your competitor, who called her for the first time last week? Unless your competitor offers some tremendous advantage or proprietary method you don't have, you stand the better chance of getting the business.

For this reason, it pays to get prospects involved with you at an early stage, even before any money is exchanged or any contracts are signed.

If you're a professional speaker, for example, send a demo tape or invite prospects to your next talk. The time prospects invest in going to see you or listening to your tape is an investment for which they won't get any return unless they ultimately hire you.

If they go to your speech or showcase presentation and don't use you, they've wasted their time, and they know it. So prospects naturally tend to want to hire the service provider they have already invested time and effort learning about, investigating, or speaking with.

In my business, freelance copywriting, instead of just sending prospects my brochure, I'll also ask certain ones to mail to me extensive background material on their companies. I tell prospects I need this material to better understand their marketing problems and how I can help them (all true).

This helps me close the sale for two reasons. First, it impresses prospects that I care enough about them to want to read and learn about their company. And second, it requires prospects to spend some time deciding what to send me, making the selection, writing a covering letter, and preparing the package for the post office or Federal Express (some, of course, can avoid this by sending me to their websites).

I believe that while making the decision to hire me, many prospects say to themselves, "Well, I already spent all that time sending him our background material, and he's already up to speed on our situation, so the easiest thing is to go with Bly." They pass over my competitor because that person isn't ready to start the job, and because they haven't invested any time briefing him.

In keeping with this strategy, many consultants offer a free initial meeting or consultation, even though their hourly rates may be substantial. Now, in such cases prospects aren't motivated to hire you because they feel guilty about wasting your time. No. Rather, they consider such an initial meeting an investment of their time, and they are afraid of wasting their time, not yours.

Think about how you can involve your prospects early. Do you survey their employees? Give them a demonstration? Get them to attend your free seminar? Have them watch a videotape? Install a system in their office for a free 30-day trial? The more time prospects invest, the more eager they will be to make sure that the relationship moves forward on a productive (and for you, a paid) basis.

Act as if You Already Have the Business

This doesn't mean you pour the foundation, write the report, conduct the seminar, do the survey, ship the merchandise, install the equipment, or start the work. That would be premature and foolish.

When I say act as if you already have the job, I mean your tone, mannerisms, and posture should exude confidence. Without being obvious or high handed, you should behave as if getting the project is a foregone conclusion, with fee negotiations, contracts, and purchase orders a mere formality standing in the way of you getting started. As writer Judy Brewerton observes, you want to get out of the "audition" mode and into a working relationship mode as soon as possible.

Most service providers handle the closing phase of the sales process awkwardly. They act as if they don't know what to do, are ashamed and embarrassed to be closing the sale, and want to give prospects sufficient time to contemplate this major decision.

Successful salespeople are confident and decisive. They feel sure enough about their abilities to say to prospects: "We are best qualified. Our service can solve your problem and do it well. What are you waiting for? Sign on the dotted line and we'll get started."

Prospects want to hire people who appear to know what they're doing. This means being a man or woman of action. It's time for prospects to move forward, but inertia, laziness, or uncertainty prevents them from doing so. They look to you for guidance. You must take prospects by the hand and gently, but forcefully, get them to commit to action.

False modesty (or maybe genuine lack of confidence) prevents many of us from acting confidently. Our attitude is "Gee, Mr. Prospect, I don't blame you for not wanting to make a decision. There are lots of people who can do what I do. And besides, it's a lot of money and I don't want you to make a rash decision. Take your time; we're in no hurry." Unfortunately, this attitude only feeds prospects' natural inertia. It will not get you the sale you want, which means prospects will not benefit from the services you provide.

Act as if you already have the job, project, or order. Your attitude should be: "Mr. Prospect, I'm happy you called me here today because I've handled many customers with needs like yours, and I know I can help you immensely. The fee is X dollars payable in these installments. I'm really looking forward to working with you!"

This attitude will subtly alter the texture of the conversation between you and prospects. Instead of being in a selling mode, you'll be in a working partnership mode. Your comments will be directed toward understanding customers' requirements or helping to find the best solution for their problems, not desperately thinking of what you can say to persuade them to give you a retainer check or sign a contract.

And when this happens, you'll perform better and close more sales. Why? Because prospects like to deal with vendors who are genuinely helpful and interested in them. They don't like to deal with vendors who are pushy and only seem interested in getting their money. When you act as if you're already on the job, you will behave as if you're in the former category, not the latter. So prospects will like you better. And you'll close more sales. Always act as if you already have the job, not as if you're auditioning or begging for it.

Success is magnetically attractive, as long as it is not demonstrated in an ostentatious fashion. Prospects will be impressed by a busy waiting room, a packed showroom, a long customer list, or a filled appointment book, all of which show that you are busy and therefore, by extension, successful.

When your symbols of success are too gaudy, you risk turning off some prospects even though you may be impressing others; why even take the chance? If your sales brochure is too elaborate and elegant, if your offices are richly furnished in priceless antiques, if your car is a luxury model light-years beyond what the prospect can afford, you may cause resentment.

I have a policy of never telling customers how much money I earn, because the answer can only hurt me. If I earn much more than the customer who is hiring me, he may suddenly find my fees unreasonable. If I earn much less, he may think I am not successful and therefore not competent at my profession. When customers press me about my earnings, I answer: "Well, I'm not Bill Gates, but I make a decent living." And I leave it at that.

Acting as if you don't need the business gives you incredible leverage in selling and negotiating situations, and actually not needing the business is even better. Howard Shenson always advised me, "Act as if you don't need the business even if you do."

The problem was, I did not have the constitution for it, and many salespeople don't either. Therefore, I have a better strategy: to always ensure, through ongoing marketing, that I really don't need the business.

I advise my clients to do constant marketing to generate a steady stream of sales leads. When you keep a full pipeline of leads, you will always have more opportunities for new business than you can handle. Therefore, you truly won't need an individual prospect, and can negotiate with them from a position of strength. It's only when you desperately need more business that you negotiate from weaknesses; your weakness comes across to the prospect and puts them, not you, in control.

Avoid "Pressure" Closings

In direct mail, having a time-limited offer is an extremely effective technique. Phrases like "Offer expires December 15," "Supplies are limited— order today!" and "This is a limited offer, and once it expires, it may never be repeated" give prospects genuine reasons to respond now instead of later, which dramatically increases response rates.

But, while most people are understanding and responsive to such time-limited offers in direct mail situations, they resent such pressure in a selling situation. For instance, when buying a car, I resent it when the salesperson tells me, "This price is good today only; if you walk out of the showroom it'll be more costly if you come back later." My response is to walk out and buy the car across the street. True, some prospects will be scared into buying the car on the spot. But this tactic makes them unhappy and resentful.

While the car salesperson may believe he can afford to make the prospect uncomfortable by using high-pressure selling—he'll probably never see the customer again, anyway—you cannot. You may be dealing with prospects on a daily or weekly basis if they become customers, so you don't want to start the relationship off on a negative note. And that's exactly what pressure selling does.

Here are a few of my "don'ts" concerning pressure selling:

- *Don't* tell prospects, "I can give you this price, but only if you commit today." This makes you look sleazy and makes prospects extremely uncomfortable.

- *Don't* tell prospects, "I'm getting extremely busy, and unless you sign up with me today, I may not be able to handle your job" unless it's the absolute truth. (If it's true, then you're doing prospects a favor by indicating to them what they must do to ensure they can get you for this project.)

- *Don't* lie or say things that prospects will not believe. If business is scarce, and you're desperate to make the sale, don't try to pressure prospects by saying, "We're very busy and we only have one slot open on our schedule, so you need to sign up this week or we won't be able to take you on." Prospects will know you are lying.

- *Don't* use two-tier pricing—that is, a low price if prospects buy today versus a higher price if prospects want to think about it and get back to you. While this works effectively in direct-mail selling, it can backfire in personal selling. Be careful.

PROSPECT REPELLANT #13:

Providing overly strong incentives for the prospect to buy today instead of tomorrow.

A "deal sweetener" is something the salesperson throws in at the last minute to close the deal when the prospect is sitting on the fence.

For instance, when selling a computer system to a small business, the computer reseller might say, "Tell you what. Let's close this deal today and I will give you free installation."

You have to be very careful when using deal sweeteners. Here's my rule of thumb: Deal sweeteners work when (a) the prospect is close

> to buying but not quite there, (b) the deal sweetener is something
> they would really like and prefer not to pay for (e.g., free installa-
> tion or free shipping), and (c) the deal sweetener has a relatively
> modest value compared to the overall purchase price.

In the example of the computer reseller, offering to install the computer system would work. The prospect would like this service (few people want to deal with the headache of installation), but probably don't want to pay extra for it. And the perceived value of an installation is relatively modest compared to the purchase price of a small business computer system.

On the other hand, say the prospect wasn't sold and was about to walk out the door. Maybe the price was too high. The computer reseller offers, as a deal sweetener, to take 20 percent off the price, or to throw in an extra workstation or two.

Instead of magnetically attracting the prospect and bringing them back to a sale, it magnetically repulses them and pushes them farther away.

Reason: When the computer reseller offers a 20 percent lower price or to throw in thousands of dollars of extra equipment, the prospect thinks: "If that's the deal, why didn't you offer it to me right away instead of when it looked like I wasn't going to buy? If I *had* bought, does that mean I would have paid 20 percent higher than the real price?"

A too-large deal sweetener, thrown in as a desperation measure to keep a prospect from walking, is seen as dishonest: The original price quoted was inflated, and therefore the seller was ripping me off.

Remove the Risk

The fastest route to overcoming buyer resistance when attempting to close a sale is to take the burden of risk off prospects' shoulders and place the risk on the shoulders of you, the seller.

For instance, if prospects resist your closing, stress the fact that they can hire you risk-free; that you will make any changes they request at no charge; that you guarantee your product for thirty days, or ninety days, or better still, for one year; that you will warrant the product against defects in materials and labor; that you stand behind customers 100 percent; that you will give more service at no cost or refund all or part of the money if you don't perform as promised.

Obviously, we can't make our guarantee *too* good, or we leave ourselves open to unscrupulous buyers who would take advantage of us. The trick is to appeal to sincere prospects with an offer that makes it as painless, easy, and risk-free as possible for them to try our goods and services. You can do this with either some sort of guarantee, warranty, or promise of performance, or by allowing prospects to buy a demo or sample before committing to a larger contract.

How do you work this into your closing technique? Let's say a prospect resists having you do her ad campaign because she's not sure if the firm really wants to switch ad agencies (despite her claim they were ready to switch when they called you in). You could ask, "Do you have any one ad that needs to be done right away?" Then offer to do the single ad on a project basis.

You'll probably close, because it's much less of a commitment for a company to hire you to do one ad than to switch their entire account to your agency. Interestingly, in the advertising business, most ad agencies I know would refuse to do this. Their attitude is "We want the whole account or nothing at all." Competitors who are more flexible and willing to allow the prospect to "sample" their services with a trial project can succeed against them in winning new business.

AFTO: Ask for the Order

Marketing and sales expert Ray Jutkins says the key to success in marketing and selling is AFTO, which stands for "ask for the order." This means if you want a signed contract, you must present a contract ready for signature and preferably, place the pen in the prospect's hand and put his hand over the blank space provided for him to sign. If you want a check, tell the customer, "Make out a retainer check for X dollars, and we'll get started."

You have to ask for the order, the assignment, the project, the contract, the agreement, the paperwork, the go ahead, the check, the purchase order, the job. If you don't, you won't get it.

At a meeting of the Wednesday Club, a group of independent PR firms based in and around New York City, owners of small PR agencies were discussing how they closed sales and got customers to put them on retainer. I asked one experienced PR man, "What do you do when the customer is ready to go and wants to know what the next step is?"

The man reached into his briefcase and pulled out a poster board. On the poster was a pasted-up copy of his agency agreement, with a big arrow and the words "SIGN HERE" (drawn in huge lettering) indicating a blank space at the bottom. "The next step," said this successful consultant, "is to get them to sign on the bottom line."

Close Quickly

When prospects indicate they are ready to buy, act fast. Immediately write up a quotation, prepare the contract, or send an agreement. Have it in the prospect's hands within 48 hours. You can send it by first-class mail, Federal Express, or, if it's just a page or two, via fax or e-mail.

Why is prompt response important? Two reasons. First, it makes sense to get prospects to commit right away. If they have too much time to think about it, they may find additional reasons for delaying or deferring. The delay may also give your competitor time to move in.

Second, prospects judge you on first impressions and form their opinion of you largely based on how you perform in the initial phases of any engagement or relationship. If you're tardy or indifferent about preparing the quotation or contract, or about getting started on the assignment, this gives prospects cause to think you'll be even less motivated and caring later on. And that's not what they want.

PROSPECT REPELLANT #14:

Not following through.

Use a contact management system such as Act or Goldmine (see Appendix A) to keep track of your prospects and when you promised to get back to them.

> For instance, if you tell the prospect, "I will call you in two weeks," you enter that date in your contact manager. When the date arrives, you get an automated reminder on the computer screen to call the prospect.
>
> Call when you said you would call. Write when you said you would right. Send the catalog, literature, proposal, or price quote on or before the day you promised.
>
> I do not leave it to chance and assume my prospects get the price quotations we e-mail them. We call after we e-mail to confirm their receipt of our estimate. This way, nothing is left to chance.

If you're not computer savvy or comfortable with writing, now is the time to improve your e-mail skills. In the age of instant messaging and e-mail, transferring information quickly doesn't mean it's done in a sloppy, unprofessional manner.

Assume every e-mail you send will be kept in a file and forwarded or shared with many different employees in your target company. Misspelled words, poor grammar, and punctuation errors shout that you haven't taken the time to put your best self forward.

Says Sally, a buyer for a bookstore, "There's nothing that turns me off faster than getting a sales letter with a misspelled word in it. I immediately think the person who sent it is careless and not attentive to the details. It tells me she's in a hurry, that my business is not worth getting the very best—from initial communication to the completed order. If she can't spell correctly in a cover letter, how can I trust that the book she's trying to sell me won't have similar errors in it?"

If you're careless in the details of communication, your customer may wonder what to expect when you have to deliver the bigger goods or services. Remember not to use e-mail to transmit important or confidential information; that should be done by letter or telephone.

Here are a few suggestions to keep in mind when corresponding with your customer:

- Begin with a friendly salutation. Unless you've been told not to do so, address your customer as Ms., Mr., or Mrs.
- The subject of your message should be stated short and clear.
- Use upper and lower case—no one wants to be shouted at through an e-mail filled with capital letters, which is difficult to read.
- Beneath your signature, list your address, phone number, and other relevant contact information.
- Respond to e-mails within twenty-four hours. If that's not a doable option, a quick phone call explaining you've read the request and will get the information together as soon as possible is in order.
- When you are away from the office without access to e-mail for more than a day, set up an "autoresponder" message that lets people know this, and gives them a phone number to call for immediate assistance.

I have been teaching on-site seminars in persuasive writing for decades. But perhaps instead of the word "persuade," which sounds heavy-handed and argumentative, the better word to use for the interaction between customer and sales representative should be "convince," which carries the connotation that you are causing someone to agree with a belief or course of action using earnest requests.

So much of what we say and how we act and react is commonsense behavior we practice in our everyday private lives. However, in the heat of the moments of the sales presentation and its subsequent close, these are things we often forget.

Brushing up on communication skills, being knowledgeable about your product or service, and believing wholeheartedly in its ability to solve problems for your customer will go a long way toward getting him or her excited about—and interested in—what you are offering.

If you want to eliminate the phrase "no, thank you" or "not right now" from your customer's response, treat your prospects the way you want to be treated: as peers looking to find a solution to make running a business efficient and more profitable. You'll not only get more sales, but you'll avoid burnout and look forward to each new business day.

Constantly Closing

When, exactly, can you consider the sale closed? When prospects call and say they're tentatively interested? When customers say, "Yes, go ahead"? When the contract is signed? When you get your advance check? Or is it when the check clears in the bank?

In one sense, the sale is never truly closed. We are constantly closing; that is, we're always striving to make sure customers are satisfied and pleased with us. We can't really consider the sale closed when we get the signed contract or purchase order, because customers can always cancel, and it may be difficult to collect all or even a portion of your fee when that happens.

One salesman confided in me, "I consider the sale made when the customer's check clears in my bank account." But even that isn't the end of it. You've got to perform as promised, or the customer might sue for return of fee based on nonperformance.

Plus, for many businesses, the one-shot customer is the least profitable. The real money is made with repeat buyers and customers who retain us on a periodic or, even better, an ongoing basis. The repeat business is where the profits are made. To get these repeat assignments, our performance on the initial job must be superior.

In a sense, everything we do or say in the course of our relationship with the customer determines whether we close that next sale. We are constantly closing this sale and the next. Selling does not end with the signed contract but is ongoing throughout the life of the consultant/customer relationship.

Let Prospects Help You Close

According to veteran salesman Tim Connor, as reported in *In Business* magazine, your prospects will tell you what you need to say to them in order to close the sale. This means you have to ask questions, get them talking, and listen to what they really want from you.

For instance, I was trying to get a prospect to retain me as a consultant to help him start up a mail-order business for an exciting new product.

Although the prospect had been enthusiastic when he called me, and maintained his enthusiasm for me throughout the meeting, I couldn't quite get him to commit to the next step: a signed contract retaining me.

Finally I said, "What's holding you back?"

The prospect said, almost reluctantly, "I believe you know what you're talking about, but all of this is new to me. I'm afraid that other vendors I need—the designer, manufacturer, printer, mail house, and list broker—will sense my novice status and take advantage of me."

Based on his statement, I understood that the cause of his reluctance was that I was a "hands-off" consultant and would not assist him with the nitty gritty details. When I assured him I could act as project manager (for a separate fee), overseeing the details and coordinating with his vendors, his anxiety disappeared and I won the contract.

Listen to your prospects. Frequently they will tell you, word for word, what they want to hear from you—indeed, what they *need* to hear from you—before they will hire you.

A technique that works well is to ask prospects what they want, then repeat it back to them in your own words. When prospects hear their requirements spoken by you, they will be confident that you truly understand what they need:

Prospect: "I need someone who can meet with our production people next week."

You: "So if we could prepare an initial briefing for your production team to be presented next week, I take it you'd be interested in proceeding with this project?"

Prospect: "Yes."

Match Closing Tactics to Buyer Mood

Another piece of good advice Tim Connor gives is that you must sell to prospects in the way they are comfortable buying, not the way you are comfortable selling. And this goes especially for the closing—a situation in which the prospect, faced with finally having to make a real decision, has the greatest level of fear and anxiety.

We've all been in situations where we haven't bought a product or service because the salesperson made us uncomfortable. To increase your chances of closing the sale, be in sync with the mood and personality of your prospects, and adjust your presentation accordingly.

For instance, people speak at an average rate of 150 words per minute. But they will speed up when calling New York City and slow down when calling Tennessee or Georgia, because they sell more effectively when the pace of their chatter matches that of the person they're calling.

In the same way, training seminars on selling overseas advise international businesspeople to follow the local business customs of the customer's country. After all, most people would rather buy from people who are like them rather than from people who are strange and different.

Now, this doesn't mean you should be a chameleon, totally changing your stripes and colors to match whatever personality you think would be ideal for selling a particular prospect. This would be phony, and people can spot a phony. However, it does pay to be sensitive to the prospect's personality and mood, and adjust your style within reason to match.

For example, if prospects seem pressed for time, compress your sales pitch to accommodate their busy schedules and get to the close quickly. On the other hand, if prospects seem relaxed, with plenty of time on their hands, you can slow down and have a more leisurely chat.

I have one customer, Shirley, who is a real gabber. She loves to talk and talk and talk. While I can't afford to let her go on indefinitely, I generally settle in for a five- or ten-minute chat.

Why not? I genuinely like Shirley. She's interesting and has a lot to say. And with the fees she pays me, I can afford to indulge her a bit—something I might not do with a smaller customer. Another customer, Randy, is a brisk, no-nonsense, to-the-point guy. Many people are turned off by Randy's brusqueness and consider him rude. Not I. We get along great, mainly because my personality is close to his.

Leo, on the other hand, was a child of the sixties and is into touchy feely interpersonal relationships. He frequently tells me what a beautiful human being I am and that he loves me. I'm not fully able to respond to Leo in the same way, because I'm not like that, and we both know it. But that's okay with us, and I am more personal and warmer with Leo than I am with Randy.

Adjust your presentation and style to the prospect's mood and personality, especially during the sensitive closing period, and you will improve your sales results and customer relationships.

The Take-Away Close

A few years ago I came across a brochure for an independent consultant, Sommers White.

The brochure promoting White's consulting services was written entirely in question and answer format. But what really caught my eye was the first Q & A in the lead:

Q: Why should I hire Sommers White?

A: Perhaps you should not.

Why is this opening so effective? First, it is unexpected. The surprise factor gets your attention. Second, it instantly builds White's credibility. Obviously, here is a guy who only wants customers he can help. He won't just take any business. He has to believe he can really help you before he will work with you. What an ethical guy!

Third, it actually enhances the desire to find out more about White and possibly hire him. It's intriguing. Who is this man of mystery? Why is he so sure of himself that he doesn't even want your business?

This technique of selling is called "the take-away close." White did not invent it, although his use of it as a lead is unusual. The basic premise of the take-away close is: People want what they can't have. Think about it. Your doctor tells you, "No more fatty food." What do you instantly want? A bacon cheeseburger!

Sales trainer Paul Karasik recommends you use the take-away method when trying to close a sale with a reluctant prospect. If the prospect is hemming and hawing, shut your notebook or folder, take the contract off the table, and say, "You know, you're right. This may not be for you."

The prospect will immediately want to know why you say this, and often, will try to prove you wrong. In essence, they'll start selling *you* on changing your mind and accepting them as a customer. What an ideal situation for you!

Another thing that makes the take-away close so effective is what I call the power of the contrary: When you do something people don't expect, it is an instant attention-getter.

A radio commercial for Seaman's, a furniture store in my area, begins: "Whatever you do, DON'T buy furniture today!" You don't expect a furniture store to tell you not to buy furniture. So you listen. It sounds like you are going to get helpful consumer advice—maybe tips on shopping for furniture. Turns out, the tip is to wait to Saturday for Seaman's big blowout sale. But it works. They got your attention—and now you want to wait for their sale.

The next time you are having trouble closing a prospect or moving a sale forward, try the take-away close. One caveat: You have to be willing to lose the sale to make this work. You must be prepared for and ready to accept the possibility that the prospect will say, "Yes, you're right, this is not for me."

Therefore, the take-away close should only be used in two situations: (a) when you already have more business than you can handle and therefore can afford to lose the sale, or (b) when the sale is stalled and you cannot move the prospect forward using your other closing techniques.

ATTRACTION PRINCIPLE #19:

The less you seem to need the business, the more desirable you become to the prospect.

Want to avoid seeming desperate or needy? Use the "take-away" close.

For example, in Somers White's sales brochure the first question is, "Why should I hire Somers White?" The unexpected answer in the brochure is: "Perhaps you should not."

The take-away close works because of this principle: Suggesting to someone that they can't have a thing makes them want it even more.

> The late Howard Shenson called this the Busy Doctor Syndrome, which he stated as follows: "Prospects would rather buy from vendors whom they perceive as busy and successful, rather than those who seem to need the work."

Become Comfortable with Closing

You may hate closing now. And although many salespeople come to love the selling and marketing aspects of their business, some never do. But most people I talk to tell me they become more at ease with selling, more comfortable with the idea of asking for the order, over time.

Here are three suggestions for putting yourself more at ease with the concept of closing:

1. Remember, the worst the prospect can do is say "no." And that's really not so terrible. There are plenty of other prospects out there for you. There's always tomorrow.

2. The situation need not be awkward or unpleasant if you maintain professional, cool, detached behavior at all times. If the prospect says "no," it doesn't mean loss of dignity or face for you. Your inner mental attitude should be, "I'd like to help you, Mr. Prospect, but if you refuse to see the wisdom of buying from us, the loss is primarily yours, not mine."

3. Most independent consultants take the position that any customer who buys from them is doing them a favor. They aren't. Think of the transaction as (in the words of Robert J. Ringer, author of *Looking Out for #1*) a "value-for-value" exchange of goods and services for money. Realize that they need you as much as you need them.

Closing When the Prospect Is Looking at Other Vendors

Here are some tips for winning business when you know the prospect is looking at other vendors:

187

- Find out what customers want and give it to them.

- Ask customers how they will be making the decision. On price? Other factors?

- Only pursue leads you have a reasonable chance of winning. If you are a premium service but you know the prospect is buying on price and also talking to your low-end competitor Joe Low-Ball, why bother even bidding?

- Offer a value or service package or a guarantee your competitors don't. According to an article in *CIO* (January 1, 1998), in those jittery pre-millennium days, Cap Gemini America, an IT consulting firm, guaranteed renovation of between 750,000 and 1.5 million lines of COBOL code in four weeks—or your money back. This set them apart from other Year 2000 consultants.

ATTRACTION PRINCIPLE #20:

If an account isn't worthwhile, don't pursue it.

Want to close every sale? Here's an easy way: Make the best product in the world, have the best service in the world and the fastest delivery, and give it away for free.

Too many businesspeople give away the store just to close business.

An account is only worthwhile if it is profitable for you—or if (in rare instances) it adds prestige, builds visibility, or brings in a ton of lucrative business through referral or word of mouth. If a customer doesn't want you to make a fair profit, he or she probably isn't a customer you want to have.

Here's an interesting phenomenon: Often when you turn potential customers away, it actually serves to intensify their desire to do business with you—to the point where they are willing to accept whatever prices, terms, and conditions you dictate.

As I mentioned earlier, telling prospects, "Maybe we are not right for you; I suggest you might be better served elsewhere" is called the take-away close: by NOT trying to sell people, you end up selling them more effectively than if you actually wanted their business.

The take-away close works because people want what they can't have. It also puts you in control, rather than the buyer: When what you sell is not easily purchased, it builds desire to own it—and prospects will actually work to convince you to give it to them. For the seller, what's better than that?

Note

1. David Ogilvy, *Confessions of an Advertising Man* (New York: Dell, 1964).

Magnetic Customer Service

Let your pledged word ever be sacred. Never promise to do a
thing without performing it with the most rigid promptness.
Nothing is more valuable to a man in business than the name
of always doing as he agrees, and that to the moment.

—P.T. BARNUM

If you've already put the principles expressed in previous chapters to work and are getting good results, you may think, "Things are pretty okay with my customers at this point; now I can relax." Not so. One of the key secrets of ensuring customer satisfaction I haven't shared with you yet is this: *diligence.*

Customer satisfaction is not something you practice one month, then coast on when things are going smoothly. It is an attitude, and a way of doing business, that must be diligently applied every waking moment, every minute of the business day.

It takes months, even years, of excellent customer service to form solid, lasting relationships with the most profitable, lucrative accounts. And all that can be destroyed with one slip, one lapse, one error that gets the buyer ticked off at you enough to make them walk.

Therefore, you can't "relax" when it comes to applying the principles of maximum customer satisfaction expressed in this book. You have to do it every week, every day, every hour, every minute. Tiring? Possibly. Doable? Yes. Rewarding? I guarantee it.

Another reason why diligently practicing maximum customer satisfaction and never "letting your guard down" is important is that, in this "Age of the Customer," only those firms that create maximum customer satisfaction will survive and prosper.

"Let's make sure that our customers are satisfied," suggests Lois Geller, president of Lois Geller Direct, in an article in *Target Marketing*. "Lack of customer service can break all of our efforts. If we are to cement buyer loyalty, customer satisfaction must be a key objective."

Low levels of customer satisfaction can cost your business a lot of money. According to investment consultant and author John M. Cali, Jr., 91 percent of unhappy customers who have been treated discourteously will not buy from the offending business again. And, just as bad, says Cali, the average unhappy customer will complain about the poor treatment you gave them to nine or ten other people, and 13 percent of these unhappy customers will tell more than twenty other people!

Succeed by Being Better, Not by Being Great

Many business authorities say the only way to succeed is by being great at everything you do. The book *In Search of Excellence* inspired a new breed of business authors, speakers, and seminar leaders, proclaiming that only "excellence" will win customers and profits in the 1990s.

While striving for excellence is a laudable goal, there are two problems I have with experts telling you you have to be great or excellent to stay in business. First, it puts tremendous pressure on you. It's hard enough today to juggle all your responsibilities and still get all your work done on time. To have to be great in everything you do as well? It's too much!

Second, it's not true. You see, to stand head and shoulders above your competition, you don't have to be "great" or "excellent," you just have to be significantly *better* than the competition.

And in giving customers good service, that's fairly easy, because—

despite all we read in the business press about the importance of customer service—many businesses are lousy when it comes to customer service. So you don't have to be great, you just have to be better than they are. And because they're so mediocre, it's easy for you to beat them.

"You beat 50 percent of the people in America by working hard," says A. L. Williams, the self-made millionaire life insurance salesman, in his book, *All You Can Do Is All You Can Do*. "You beat another 40 percent by being a person of honesty and integrity and by standing for something. The last 10 percent is a dogfight in the free-enterprise system."

ATTRACTION PRINCIPLE #21:

Build long-term relationships, not short-term sales.

A supermarket manager refused to give a customer a refund on a bag of spoiled shrimp because she didn't have the receipt. "How do I know the shrimp wasn't fresh when you left the store?" he said to the customer. "Maybe you forgot to refrigerate the shrimp, and it spoiled, and I'm not going to be ripped off for $13!" He saw $13 of precious sales revenue at risk—and acted accordingly by refusing a refund.

He should have given the refund—even though she didn't have the receipt. Reason: If the customer spends $100 a week at the store, her business is worth more than $5,000 a year. Would you want to lose a $5,000 account over a $13 complaint?

Base your selling efforts on potential lifetime customer value, not the one-shot sale—and act accordingly.

The amateur salesperson is concerned only with the immediate sale: the revenue and commission he can get by getting the customer to buy a single product.

The professional salesperson is busily calculating the potential "lifetime customer value" of each account.

Lifetime customer value refers to how much money the customer is likely to spend with your business during the period while he remains an active customer.

Say your average unit of sale is $200. Your average customer makes three purchases a year, and remains a customer for 5 years. Multiply all that out, and the average lifetime customer value is $3,000.

When you base the time, effort, and money you spend to win new business on the total lifetime customer value, you gain a substantial advantage over competitors who base their effort and expenditure on just the first sale. After all, who's going to make more of an effort to win a new customer: the salesperson who sees a $200 sale or the salesperson who sees a $3,000 sale?

Your understanding of lifetime customer value changes your whole perception of what you can afford to spend—in time and effort—to acquire a new customer. When you see a potential customer as a $3,000 revenue stream instead of a $200 sale, you automatically take your selling to a whole new level proportionate with the greater reward you will receive for closing.

Get Your Customers to Trust You

Use good manners in all interactions with your customers. Be polite, cool, calm, and collected. In today's society, acting busy and harried has become almost a status symbol. Yet customers resent it when you are curt with them, or act as if their call is an annoyance or interruption, or make them feel you don't have time for them.

An article in the *Record* (1/6/92) reports that in a survey of 200 businesspeople, bad manners were the number one complaint among those surveyed. People don't like to be treated rudely. So don't do it. Take the time to be polite and give each customer your full attention, acting as if their concern and problem is your number one priority and the only thing you have to deal with that day.

> **ATTRACTION PRINCIPLE #22:**
>
> **You can't predict or control how customers react. You can only be prepared to respond to whatever action they take.**
>
> "You can't be responsible for other people," a wise person once said. "You can only be responsible to them."

> Or, as journalist Sydney Harris put it, "You will never win an argument with an irrational human being."
>
> Most people are rational. A few are not. If you believe you never should or never will have "people problems" in your life, you are bound to be disappointed.
>
> Psychologist Edward Honan advises seeing problems as nothing more than "a bump in the road." When there is a bump in the road, you go over it or around it. You don't spend weeks fuming about it, nor do you take it as a personal offense.
>
> Recognize that a small percentage of customers will be irrational, difficult, cantankerous, rude, fussy, and otherwise objectionable. Don't react in kind; react with kindness. As Dale Carnegie once said, "If you want to gather honey, don't kick over the beehive."

If you are employed by a company, your sales manager will dictate with whom you have to work. When you encounter a prospect you cannot abide, suggest to the sales manager that this prospect is not worth the effort—or ask that he be assigned to another salesperson.

Those of us who are self-employed enjoy greater freedom in our ability to choose who we will work with, and the key to a happy life is to exercise this freedom. Life is too short to deal with idiots. "Fire" problem customers and turn difficult prospects away, as soon as your financial situation allows you to do so.

When you begin to do this, you become magnetically attractive to everyone around you. People like and are attracted to us when we are confident enough to dictate the tone of our relationships.

Don't fawn over people or pursue relationships too vigorously or ardently. If people sense that you like but don't need them, they find this much more attractive than if you were needy. "Independence" makes people magnetically attractive, while "neediness" does the opposite.

When a customer or prospect does something hurtful—a rejection, rudeness, arrogance, a dressing down—don't take it personally or let it erode your self-esteem. You are not responsible for other people's actions; only they are responsible for those actions. If they act inappropriately, why should that make you feel badly about yourself?

Listen to Your Customers

Failure to listen is usually caused by eagerness to be speaking. When you find yourself cutting off the other person's sentences, and not listening but sitting there waiting for them to finish so you can talk, you're not really listening. And that's bad—for two reasons.

First, if you don't listen, you don't know what the customer really wants you to do; therefore, you can't do it. And if you don't do what the customer wants, you don't have a satisfied customer.

Second, it annoys the customer. If they see you are not listening, they will feel you are not interested in them and their problems. Equally as important as listening is to let the customer know you are listening. This is done by making eye contact, sitting in an attentive position, leaning forward slightly to signal your intense interest, and by brief verbal responses that show you are paying attention ("I understand," "That's interesting," "Really?" "Uh-huh," "Tell me more," etc.).

Another useful technique is, after the customer is done speaking, to pause for a full second or two before you begin your reply. If you jump in too soon, the customer may get the false impression that you weren't really listening and were just "waiting for your turn" to speak. By pausing for a second or two, you convey the impression that you have listened carefully and are still formulating your response.

PROSPECT REPELLANT #15:

Not treating your customers with respect.

Today, people want to do their own research and make their own choices. They are busy decision makers, who do not have time to hear a sub-par presentation or be talked down to in any way.

No matter whether you are speaking to a residential customer who may want to hire your lawn service or talking with the bank president about new security systems, it is important to treat each person you encounter with dignity and respect.

"I remember the first time I walked into a new car showroom to buy my first car," says Joanna, who is now a successful sales representative for a Fortune 500 company. "Although I was only twenty years old, I had done my homework about the car I was interested in purchasing.

"Instead of treating me as he would an older, more experienced buyer, the salesman's first question to me was 'Now little lady, what color car would you like to have?' And although I would've eventually gotten around to that, I was very insulted that he assumed that would be the only thing I'd be interested in.

"That one experience clouded my opinion about car salesmen—thirty years later, I'm still expecting to hear another lame line when I walk into the showroom floor."

The first time your phone call is answered or you step through your contact's office door, the initial impression of your company is made. And it can be a lasting one as evidenced by Joanna's car buying experience.

Here are some common pet peeves you may hear about the business of sales:

- I don't like when a salesperson explains things to me as if I were totally ignorant.
- It bothers me when I'm asking a question and the salesman interrupts me with the answer before I'm finished.
- Telemarketers who call my unlisted number.
- A salesperson I've known for all of two minutes who acts as if she's been my best friend for years.
- People who will BS me just because they want my sale.
- People who call me on the phone and make it so obvious from their tone of voice that they're reading a script.
- I think it's very rude when a sales rep doesn't respect my time and continues to ramble on about his product or service.

- I don't like it when a salesperson comes on too strong. I can tell by the body language if the person is relaxed and confident or aggressive and manipulative.
- I don't want to bargain so don't tell me what you'll do for me if I give you my business.
- It drives me crazy when I spend my valuable time with a sales rep and he forgets to get back to me with the information I requested in our initial meeting.
- I can't stand it when someone won't take no for an answer. If I say "maybe in a month or two," I mean thirty or sixty days—not next week. If I haven't called you back, it's because I'm not interested.

After reading the above statements, you might be patting yourself on the back because you have not acted this way with a prospective customer. But consider this: In addition to what you say or don't say, your body is speaking another language all together.

Think about the last negative experience you had with a salesperson. Do any of these descriptions sound familiar?

- He was sitting on the edge of the chair almost leaning over my desk. Things would have gone much better if he'd have been relaxed and appeared confident. Instead I felt he was being very aggressive and this immediately made me resist what he was trying to sell me.
- The sales rep showed up at my office a half hour early and was so damned perky she drove my poor receptionist crazy. No one is that cheery at any hour—and even if you are—tone it down.
- Small talk drives me crazy! Build a relationship with me and my company—not a phony rapport based on a ten-minute surface conversation. Just because we both golf at the same course doesn't mean I'm going to commit a large order to you.

Even the most honest salesperson can make a blunder that will cause things to go south in a hurry. Have you done—or have you been on the receiving end of—any of the following failed sales techniques?

- You appear overly eager and use continuous enthusiastic, affirmative responses. By doing that, you end up sounding unbelievable. Why? Because people involved in normal day-to-day conversation don't sound that way. They'd answer a question with a simple phrase, such as "Sure, we could do that" or "I think it might work better for you this way."

- As you end your presentation, you lean forward and, in a lower voice, say to your customer, "Listen George, I'll do whatever it takes to get your business." Now if George isn't your decision maker, if he's just your gateway to the person who can approve your proposal, you've set yourself up for failure. And if he is the man who signs the check, you'll lose his respect because you came off sounding as if you're begging for his business.

- You've landed an appointment with the number one prospective customer on your list. In your eagerness to make the sale, you exaggerate the benefits your product can deliver. You make the benefits sound so good, in fact, that Mr. Decision Maker now doubts you'll be able to deliver on your promises.

Don't lie to get the order. Experienced decision makers can spot a phony a mile away. If your customer asks for something you can't provide, be up front about it. By promising more than what you're capable of delivering or exaggerating the benefits, you're doomed to be shown the door—without a sales order in hand.

Reduce Your Customer's Dependence on You

This advice may sound contrary to common sense; after all, the more dependent a customer is on your service, the more he'll use you, and the more money you'll make, right?

But if you deliberately attempt to make a customer dependent on you, limit his growth, and not teach him to do for himself, he'll resent it. He'll see that you are trying to maximize your profit and take as much money out of his pocket as you can. And this will cause unhappiness, dissatisfaction, and distrust of you.

Doing the opposite—helping customers become less dependent on your services, not more—makes good sense. If you can show the customer how to do more for themselves, you save them money, and that's one of the primary benefits customers look for from any service provider. The less they have to spend on outside services, the more they save; the more they save, the more they'll be grateful to you. And that gratitude translates to loyalty.

What's more, reducing customer dependence on your services can actually increase use of services rather than decrease them and raise revenues instead of lower them. How? When customers do more on their own, they save money by handling routine and less critical tasks in-house. With the savings, they will have extra money to spend on more important projects and goals and are likely to think of hiring you to handle those assignments in return for your good service and honesty.

Guarantee Your Work for Your Customer

A guarantee helps build sales and buyer satisfaction. Observe that when you get a direct mail solicitation for a book, magazine subscription, or product, it usually offers a 30-day money-back trial period. Do you see why this is necessary? Without such a money-back guarantee, many consumers would not buy the product sight unseen, fearing that if they didn't like it once they received it and looked it over, they'd be stuck. A guarantee of satisfaction removes that barrier and increases sales.

If you sell a service and not a product, you have an extra difficulty: unlike manufacturers, who if they refund money can resell the products that are returned to them, once you render a service, you can never get back the time spent performing the task for the customer.

For this reason, many service providers reject the concept of a guarantee, saying, "If I give a money-back guarantee, customers will take advantage of me. They will ask me to do the service, get the benefits of the service, then say they are not happy, ask for their money back, and rip me off. So I won't do it."

Yet experience contradicts this belief. The facts are that (1) most people are honest and won't abuse a guarantee privilege, (2) having a guarantee is becoming increasingly important in getting people to buy services, and (3) customers like service providers who give a guarantee.

A guarantee shows that you are dedicated to delivering the best service possible and that you have confidence in your ability to do so. When the customer sees you are confident enough in yourself to guarantee your service, the customer becomes much more confident in—and comfortable with—you.

What types of guarantees can service businesses offer? Here are just a few of the ways to structure a service business guarantee. Feel free to use these as is or adapt them to your particular business and service.

The one thing you cannot ethically do is absolutely *guarantee* a result or service unconditionally. For example, if you are a roofer, you can guarantee the roof against leaks for twenty years, saying that if it does leak, you will repair it at no cost. But you cannot guarantee that the roof will never leak. That is simply impossible. John Cali says it best: "It's true you can't guarantee a service you provide. But you can guarantee customer satisfaction."

The strongest guarantee is to tell the customer you guarantee a good result and that if it is not achieved, the customer doesn't pay. A variation of this "guaranteed results or you don't pay" offer is the service firm whose fee is a percentage of the profits or revenues generated, or money saved, by the service.

For example, I met an inventory management consultant whose services cut costs and whose fee is 3 percent of the money saved. Under this arrangement, of course, the customer does not pay a penny unless money is actually saved; thus again, there is no risk.

You can offer a money-back guarantee based on satisfaction. This is similar to the previous guarantee, except instead of pegging the money-back guarantee on a specific result (e.g., "90 percent of participants will rate it excellent," "roof will not leak," etc.), you peg it to more subjective customer criteria.

For instance, a company that specializes in logo design makes this offer:

It will come in and do three preliminary logo designs for you at no up-front cost; if you like one and want to use it, the company negotiates a fee based on use. "If you don't like it and don't want to continue with us, we shake hands, part as friends, and you do not owe us a cent," states the owner.

The customer's satisfaction is guaranteed, and even better from the customer's point of view, they are the only judge of whether the service was satisfactory—no ifs, ands, buts, or conditions.

Or, you can offer a money-back guarantee based on performance. If you are unwilling to offer a money-back guarantee based on results achieved or customer satisfaction, a weaker but still effective pledge is to guarantee performance of service. This works especially well in industries where service providers routinely do not perform everything they promised, do not keep to schedule, or have lots of cost overruns added to the final bill (examples include defense contracting and home remodeling).

Such a guarantee might be: "We promise to do what we said, when we said it, at the price we quoted. If not, if we don't do what we said, fail to meet our deadline, or don't stick to our original estimate, then you don't pay us. Period."

Another alternative is to offer a money-back or replacement or service redo warranty. A warranty is a guarantee of satisfaction for an extended period—typically one year—after the service has been performed and the bill has been paid. In a money-back warranty, the service provider guarantees the quality of the work for the warranty period, with a refund of all or part of the money if the work doesn't stand up.

For example, an exterminator might say, "We guarantee your hotel to be free of bugs for one full year. If at any time pests reappear, we will re-treat at no charge and refund part of your exterminating fee in proportion to how long you had the reinfestation."

We recently had our tiny front lawn landscaped, for the sum of $5,500. The landscaping came with this simple guarantee: All plants guaranteed to thrive for one year or replacement is free. In fact, three bushes did die within the warranty period and were promptly replaced.

But that's not the end of the story. One of the replacement bushes died a few months after planting, and by that time, the warranty period of one year had passed. We called the landscaper to tell him the bush had died, and he said, "No problem, we'll plant something different and see if it does better; no charge, of course."

Although he had a legal right to charge us, he didn't. Isn't that what you'd want from your landscaper? Isn't that what your customers want from you?

Don't Chase Customers for Money

This is a small matter, but sometimes, it's little things that make the difference. I feel you should not be too eager to push a bill on a customer after service is completed and the money is due. Why is this?

The delivery of the product, or the completion of the service, is a very positive thing. It's what the customer wanted, and if you have delivered it, they're going to be happy. But the bill—the money they have to pay—is a negative thing. It's the one part of the deal the customer would love not to have to keep if this was possible. Money is in short supply these days, everyone is on a budget, and people don't like to part with it. So getting the final bill, and seeing that big number under "AMOUNT DUE," converts the smile into a frown.

As a result, I recommend you do not rush to bill the customer, but instead wait a short period, for three reasons:

First, the waiting period gives customers time to enjoy the fruits of your labors before having to get to the reality of paying for it. Letting them "live" with the completed project or job for a bit allows them to enjoy it and therefore raises their satisfaction level to a new high.

Second, if you bill too quickly, you risk having customers receive an invoice before you know whether they are pleased and happy or whether they want some adjustments or alterations. If customers get billed immediately, and the job is not 100 percent to their liking, their attitude will be, "I'm not going to pay one penny until she gets back here and does it right!" Having the bill will act as a magnifying glass, focusing the customer's attention on what's wrong (versus what's right) and making any minor dissatisfactions seem larger than they are.

Third, when your bill arrives two seconds after the job is done, you convey the impression that you don't really share in the customer's interest in the project or enthusiasm for the work; you remind them that you're just a hired hand, in it for the money and waiting with your hand out to be paid.

Of course, you don't want to hold up billing too long; this deprives you of cash flow and may be problematic for the customer's accounting department. But it's better to err on the side of billing too slowly than billing too quickly.

How long after the service is performed should you bill? In my consulting work, I send the bill about a week *after* I have handed in the report, given the speech, or presented the seminar to the customer.

If your "deliverable" to the customer is a report, drawing, sketch, design, computer disk, or other material to be mailed or delivered to the customer, do not enclose your invoice with your completed work. Instead, mail it in a separate envelope, and mail it *after* the customer has received your completed assignment.

Getting your work, if it's good, will make the customer happy. Don't weaken that moment of peak customer satisfaction by adding a negative element (the big bill he must pay) to the package.

If your work is done on-site, don't insist on a check before you walk away; just bill the customer net thirty days (or whatever your terms are). And don't, as so many contractors do, hang around awkwardly without saying anything, hoping the customer will "get the hint" and cough up a check.

Customers resent this behavior; it seems petty and annoying. My advice is to let them praise you for a job well done, thank them, go back to your office, write out an invoice, wait a few days, then put it in the mail.

Your accountant or bookkeeper will tell you that this advice is nonsense and will weaken your cash flow. But accounts receivables are *not*, contrary to what your accountant tells you, your firm's number one asset. *Satisfied customers are.* It won't kill you to wait another week for your money or contend with an occasional slow-payer. It will harm you far more to leave every job on a negative note and have your customers report your money-grubbing, self-centered behavior to other potential customers.

Ease Existing Customers Gradually into New Business Policies

When you notify a customer of a change in policy, procedure, or fees, do it in a way that implies this is a suggested change only, and subject to discussion or negotiation. For example, if you are sending out an announcement saying your billing procedure is changing from net 30 to net 15 days, add a paragraph to the notice that says something like:

> *We are putting this policy in place because slow payments from large corporate customers to small vendors like us put us in a cash flow crunch, makes us end up being your "banker" (a business we're not in), and would force us to raise rates to compensate. We feel the new net 15 days is a good solution for us and for you. But, of course, our policies are flexible and tailored to each customer's needs; if net 15 days is a problem for you, let us know and we'll work out an alternative.*

When you send a policy or procedure change notice to a customer and write it as a commandment etched in stone rather than a desired request that can be negotiated, you risk having customers who do not like the policy or cannot comply with the procedure leave you, without even telling you. You want to keep the lines of communication open and let the customer know you are flexible and are willing to accommodate their requirements.

Always Put the Customer First

Mark Maraia says failure to act in your customers' best interest at all times undermines their trust in you. And he is right.

Customers resent it strongly when they hear or even sense anything in your manner, behavior, or conversation indicating (1) that their interests are not your number one priority, or (2) that your self-interest, schedule, profit, problems, or concerns should in any way be of concern to the customer or have any affect on the work you are doing for that customer.

According to Dr. Rob Gilbert, "The Golden Rule–'Do unto Others What You Want Them to Do for You'–is wrong." To achieve maximum customer satisfaction, he says, you must do unto others what they want you to do for them.

Whenever you are faced with a decision whose outcome favors either you or the customer, choose the action that most benefits the customer, not you. In the short term, the customer will be the winner. In the long term, you both will.

ATTRACTION PRINCIPLE #23:

Prospects buy because they feel comfortable. They don't buy when they are made uncomfortable.

Focus on what the prospect needs, wants, and likes—not what you need, want, and like. For instance, don't cajole an unathletic prospect into playing softball with you. Don't take an introverted prospect sailing with your family for the weekend. Go into your prospects' comfort zones, rather than force them into yours.

A common mistake that salespeople make, says sales trainer Tom Hopkins, and a turn-off to the prospect, is when they voice their opinion, instead of asking prospects for their opinion.

For instance, salespeople frequently say things like, "I really like the fact that it can dice vegetables." But the prospect doesn't care what you like, and so this statement may trigger a negative response.

Similarly, stock brokers often try to convince customers to invest in a stock by saying, "You know, I've got some shares of this company in my own portfolio." Customers don't see what that has to do with their own investment decisions, since their financial circumstances are different.

Focus on what the prospect thinks, likes, and wants. Understand what author Michael Masterson calls the prospect's "core buying complex"—that bundle of emotions and impulses that drive the buying decision.

Remember the old adage: People buy based on emotion, not logic. Or at least emotion causes them to want to buy, and then they use logic to justify the decision to actually do so.

The Magic of Being Cooperative

More than almost anything else, the customer wants you to be cooperative, not difficult; easy to work with, not hard to get along with; a team player, not a prima donna.

Lou Weiss of Specialty Steel & Forge in Leonia, New Jersey, says, "What works today is a 'can-do' attitude. What the customer wants to hear you say is, 'Yes, we can do it,' not, 'No, we don't do that.'" The can-do attitude has helped Lou build several successful businesses.

In terms of communicating to the customer that you are cooperative and flexible, not difficult or unwilling to extend yourself on their behalf, there are two words that are pure magic: No problem. Here are some examples of how to put these magic words to work making your customers happy with you:

Customer: "We need it by Tuesday."

You: "No problem."

Customer: "Our budget is limited on this project."

You: "No problem."

Customer: "I'll be in meetings all week, but this is important. Would it be possible for us to have a short phone conference over the weekend?"

You: "No problem."

The one thing a busy and harried customer does not want to hear when making a request is you telling him you can't do it and then going into a long explanation of the reasons why. Will there be times you cannot agree to a customer's request and legitimate reasons why you cannot do so? Of course. And at those times you will have to say no and explain why.

The idea is to reduce to a minimum the number of occasions on which you tell a customer "no." You do this by being flexible, by putting the customer's interests above your own, by being customer focused, and by realizing you are in a service business, and that service (according to the *American Heritage Dictionary*) means "work done for others," with the emphasis on *others*.

Often doing all the things you agree to do for your customers means working harder and putting in more hours. Many businesspeople complain to me, "It's not fair; I have to work much harder now than I did ten or twenty years ago." Well, if it were easy, everybody would be doing it. So quit complaining, buckle down, and get to work!

It is *other people*—your customers—you must please to succeed in your business. You want to be saying "yes" to customer requests if at all possible; those repeated "yeses" and "no problems" are what make customers love dealing with you.

While an occasional "no" is sometimes necessary, turning down a customer is something you want to avoid at almost any cost. As one sharp business owner said to me, "Every 'no' to a customer initiates a search on the customer's part for another vendor to do the job you turned down, and that gives your competition a prime opportunity to get their foot in the door and show the customer what they can do—which is often as good as what you can do, only faster and at lower cost."

So have the can-do, no-problem attitude. Make "yes" your routine response to customer queries; get "no" out of your vocabulary. This is one of the most important elements contributing to your success.

How to Handle Unexpected Requests

The one area where most businesses fall down is when customers hit us with the unexpected. Most of us can give reasonably good service when dealing with customers on a "business as usual" basis. But when the customer asks us something out of the ordinary, we often make mistakes and end up infuriating rather than pleasing the customer.

Why is this so? It's simple. When the customer makes an unexpected request, it is usually something we don't want to do, don't know how to do, or don't know whether we can do. We don't know how to respond.

But, because it's our customer and we are his vendor, we don't want them to think that we've never encountered this situation before or that we don't know what we're doing. We also believe they are expecting a response on the spot.

As a result, we feel compelled to answer immediately, without giving the matter any thought. Since we don't know the answer, and haven't thought about it, we have to make up our answer as we go along. In doing so, we give a poor answer—one that doesn't adequately address the question.

The customer indicates that the answer isn't satisfactory or doesn't make sense. We become defensive, and argue back, trying to support a solution to a problem that we hadn't given five seconds' thought to. By arguing, we engage in an adversarial, confrontational conversation with the customer, which is always a losing proposition for the service provider and a turn-off for the customer.

How do you avoid this awful situation? The technique is simple. Instead of trying to answer the unexpected question, solve the unfamiliar problem, or handle the unusual situation on the spot, you first tell the customer you want to make sure you understand the question or the request. Ask them clarifying questions. Then repeat back their request to them in your own words, and ask if you have it right, for example, "Is that what you are looking for?"

When they say yes, you say, "That's an interesting challenge. I don't have an answer for you off the top of my head. I've had similar requests, but nothing exactly like that. Tell you what. Let me give it some thought and get back to you first thing tomorrow morning (or later today, or whatever). How does that sound?"

Then, you get off the phone or out of the meeting, go back to your office, work through the unusual request, come up with a solution and some alternatives, then call, meet with, or fax the customer to go over your proposal, and find a solution that meets her needs.

The advantages of this technique are that:

- First, it produces a superior solution to the customer's problem.
- Second, rather than make you look dumb because you couldn't answer on the spot (as many service providers fear), it makes you look smart. The customer respects that you care enough about her to handle a difficult request and quickly formulate some solutions and alternatives.
- Third, it eliminates the pressure of having to give an immediate an-

swer to a request you don't know how to handle. It buys you the extra time to do it right.

- Fourth, it comes across as cooperative and helpful, eliminating the confrontational, adversarial situation of not answering correctly, proposing something off the top of your head the customer doesn't like and then having to defend it, or saying "no" to the customer when you really didn't have to, just because you didn't see a way to handle the request within two seconds after you heard it.

PROSPECT REPELLANT #16:

Solving the prospect's problem without knowing what the problem is.

A telemarketer recently called me to sell me custom-imprinted folders. He began his pitch, with no preamble, with this question: "Mr. Bly, if I could show you a way to reduce your imprinted folder costs by 50 percent, well—you'd be interested, wouldn't you?"

I replied: "No, because I don't use custom-imprinted folders."

Total silence. His sale was dead in the water. And, he looked stupid; I was embarrassed for him.

Here's a better way to begin a cold call: "Mr. Bly, do you use custom-imprinted folders in your business?"

If I answered "yes," then his question about cost savings makes total sense and is pretty likely to be a winner. If I say "no," then I am not a prime prospect for the offer.

Too many salespeople offer benefits without knowing whether the prospect is interested in those benefits. And your prospects are turned off when you make assumptions about them that aren't true, from something as big as whether they are liberal or conservative, or as small as whether they buy imprinted folders.

The old joke about assumptions is "When you ASSUME, you make an

ASS of U and ME." There's no reason to assume anything, when you can get the answer by simply asking.

In his book, *The New Science of Getting What You Want*, Doug D'Anna writes:

> *I often think of myself not so much as a salesman, but a problem solver. During 90 percent of my "sales calls"' I'm not selling anything. I'm establishing a relationship. I do that by offering a few nuggets of free advice (sort of my free trial offer). I never push my point of view on anyone. I take the long view and try to win them over to continue to take my phone calls. Once I've done this, they have already become a customer and getting them to sign a contact is just the natural course of events.*
>
> *Had I "gone for the throat" in my first telephone call—or worse, talked about ME instead of their problems—they might not want to talk to me again. Yet, by talking about how I can solve their problems and giving them a solid solution I am offered a contract the first time I call.*[1]

Put Yourself in the Customer's Shoes

One strategy that saved me a lot of anger and frustration and made me feel better about customers (as well as treat them better) was this simple philosophy: Always look at things from your customer's point of view.

Doing this is easy, but most of us don't, because it takes a deliberate effort. For example, when faced with any decision involving our work for a customer, we tend to make an instant decision, because we're pressed for time.

Before making any decision or responding to any request involving the customer, do this. Stop, take a breath, hold it for a second, exhale slowly, and then repeat the process two more times.

Now that you are relaxed, say to yourself, "Let me look at this from the customer's point of view. If I were the customer, how would I want to be treated in this situation?" Once you have the answer, you know what to do:

Do unto the customer what the customer wants you to do. For example, a few days ago a customer asked me to fax short write-ups of seminars I was scheduled to present for her. Yesterday, under extreme deadline pressure, I got a call from her. "This isn't what I asked for," she complained.

My immediate reaction was to get testy; it was exactly what she had asked for. These were the "boilerplate" write-ups I send to everyone who hires me to speak, and no one else complained. Instead, I took a breath, and thought to myself, "If I were in her shoes, I'd probably be frantically trying to pull a big conference together in a short time, and under that enormous workload, I'd need total cooperation from vendors, no speakers giving me 'grief.'"

I said pleasantly and apologetically, "I'm sorry, Fran, that these weren't what you needed. Tell me what you need and I'll e-mail it over to you. Would noon be soon enough?" This put her at ease, made me look good, and made her feel good about having hired me. What she wanted was simple and easy to do, and I did it.

As another example, I sell business books, audio cassettes, and special reports by mail. On the shorter reports, there is no money-back refund, and this is stated on the order form. The other day, I received a letter from a buyer saying, "I like the books but not these two reports. I am returning them. Please refund my $14. I apologize about the dog-eared condition, but this is how they arrived."

My immediate reaction? (I was having a bad day.) "If he doesn't realize the tremendous value of these reports, and how he could put this information to work, he'll never succeed at his venture. And besides, there's no refund on reports." I wanted to send a letter saying, "No refunds on reports; sorry."

But that would have created a dissatisfied customer who might tell ten to twenty other people, and would never buy from me again. Who wants that? Instead, I thought, "If I were him, and I didn't like the reports, of course I would want my money back; $14 is a lot of money to waste on something you don't want."

I wrote back that I was sorry he did not like the reports, would happily give him a refund, and would give him, in addition, one free report of his choice for his trouble. How do you think that made him feel about me and my catalog?

Give credit to others who deserve it. Don't claim that you alone are the source of everything good.

Let's say you got several orders from Tom in purchasing. Tom recommends you to Dan in materials management.

The mediocre salesperson sits down with Dan and says, "By putting in my system, I reduced your operating costs 10 percent."

The great salesperson sits down with Dan and says, "Tom spent a lot of time researching systems. The one he implemented that we helped him with cut your company's operating costs by 10 percent."

Give credit where credit is due. Saying you are the sole source of all good things is not only inaccurate, but it's also not credible. "The more you say you are not a guru or rainmaker, the greater your credibility," says stockbroker Andrew Lanyi.

Others will disagree with this, but I advise you not to be egotistical or boastful. Do not say how great or wonderful you are. It's much better to let others say it for you.

I am uncomfortable talking about myself and hate to boast; I was taught that modesty is a virtue. So I always hated it when people asked me, "Why should we hire you to write our marketing materials instead of your competitors?"—because I felt it forced me to brag.

My solution was to collect over the years a huge number of testimonials from customers saying how much they liked my copy, the results it achieved for them, and how easy I was to work with. Then I simply posted the entire collection—page after page—on a section labeled "Testimonials" on my website.

The other day, a prospect balked at a price I quoted. "I can hire other copywriters at half that price," he told me. "Why are you worth that much?"

I replied, "Go to my website www.bly.com and click on Testimonials. That's why." He did so, and was silent for a few seconds as he read. Then he spoke: "Okay, I see why," he said.

Respect the Customer's Time

We've discussed how busy people are and therefore how you must respect their time. One important way to communicate this respect is always to show up on time for meetings.

Because being on time is important, plan your travel so you will arrive early for your scheduled appointment; you might leave even earlier if you expect heavy traffic or don't know the area and might get lost. Ideally, you should arrive five to ten minutes before your scheduled appointment.

This benefits the customer, because they can start on time with you. It benefits you, giving you a few minutes to get yourself together and mentally prepare. When you arrive with seconds to spare or minutes late, you often lose your composure and start the meeting in a highly agitated state.

If you think you are going to be late, call and let the customer know before you leave or from the road. If you're going to be very late, explain why and offer to reschedule at the customer's convenience (most will tell you to come anyway).

Act Above and Beyond the Call of Duty

The rule here is: When there is a problem or crisis with a job you are doing for a customer, your normal rules, procedures, and business policies do not apply, and you should do whatever it takes to solve the problem, meet the deadline, and set the situation right.

Jack Gribben, retired founder of Sun Graphics, a successful printing company, tells this story:

I had kept part of the order off a shipment, because the quality was not quite right. However, I wanted to meet my promised delivery date, so I chartered a plane for $64 (this was many years ago) to deliver the material in person from our plant to the customer the next day—even *though the fee we were charging the customer to do this portion of the printing job was only $3.50."*

Joe Vitale, coauthor of *The Joy of Service*, offers these five tips for building customer satisfaction with superior service[2]:

1. Show your appreciation to good customers. Tell the customer you appreciate their business.
2. Reward your customers. Give them something free. They may hire you for one service, but toss in something else.
3. Be friendly with your customers. And treat them well.
4. Don't let your customers wander away. Keep them loyal. If you give them everything they want, and more, they won't leave.
5. If your customers are complaining, check it out. Don't hush them. They probably want you to take care of something.

Do Your Customers Small Personal Favors

From time to time your customers will ask for small personal favors that really do not relate to your business relationship or the work you are doing for them. My feeling is, as long as the favors aren't illegal, immoral, unethical, or unreasonable, you should do them if you can.

For example, after a meeting, a customer, knowing I write books, said, "Bob, I hope you don't mind me asking, but I have an idea for a book and I think it would really sell. Do you have any advice on how to get it published?"

I mailed him several how-to reports I've written on how to get books written and published and also gave him half a dozen names of agents, editors, and publishers. Did this increase my business with them? Not visibly. Did it increase my goodwill with this particular person at the customer organization? I hope so, but don't know. Would ignoring the request and not responding have been noticed and created negative feelings from this person? I strongly believe so.

So when a customer asks, "Can you do me a favor?" don't ignore it, and don't say yes and then not follow through, hoping they will forget. They won't. Instead, say yes, then follow up immediately—as if this were a paying assignment—and do the favor you promised.

Even those favors that do not seem to pay off immediately for you create goodwill that cannot possibly hurt and that may pay off handsomely in the future. For instance, I did several favors for one customer who never reciprocated, gave me little business, and ultimately left the company and took a job out of state. But a year later, he referred two people to me, both of whom instantly became paying customers. So what goes around does come around.

This is an important concept, but keep in mind that you don't have to do everything that a customer asks you to do. You need to set boundaries.

ATTRACTION PRINCIPLE #25:

You don't have to do something just because a customer asks you to do it. People are not attracted to lackeys.

Learn to say "no." Many salespeople live in terror of saying "no" to customers. In fact, you would be amazed at how accepting customers are when you say it. You don't have to do half the things you think you have to. Learn to say "no."

Our natural intuition is to expect that saying "no" will anger people, and therefore we avoid it when dealing with bosses, customers, and others who pay our salary. But counterintuitively, people often respect you more when you set and enforce clear boundaries for relationships.

When setting boundaries, you can retain the customer's goodwill and respect by offering alternatives. For instance, if you are not in the office weekends and yours is a business where people may need to reach you outside of normal business hours, you could either give prospects your home phone number or promise to check your office voice mail once or twice each day on Saturdays and Sundays.

Notes

1. Doug D'Anna, *The New Science of Getting What You Want* (Lombardi, 2004).
2. Joe Vitale, *The Joy of Service* (Awareness Publications, 1989).

CHAPTER 13

How to Attract Referrals
Like a Magnet

The best sales leads—meaning those most likely to close—are referrals from satisfied customers. This chapter presents a simple method for magnetically pulling from your satisfied customers more referrals than you could ever hope to handle.

Why Bother with Referrals?

Lots of businesspeople are shy about asking for referrals. So their first question to me is, "Why even bother getting them?" Answer: Because referred leads usually have the highest conversion rate to sale.

Why do referral leads outperform cold prospecting lists? With all the schemes and scams occurring today, people are naturally and rightfully cautious of strangers, especially those who use cold calls to generate sales. You might have the best product or service on the market, but chances are you're still going to have a rough go of trying to engage people in positive sales dialogue. Why? Because they don't know you.

When you were a child, chances are one of the first things you learned was "Never talk to strangers." This rule sticks with many of us as we go about our daily lives—and comes into play especially when someone we don't know calls to sell us a product or service.

Immediately the guard goes up. As you're the caller and you don't hear the receiver slam in your ear, you may still hear a terse "I'm not interested," or a host of other excuses to cut the call short.

"One thing that really bugs me," says Al Pearson, a computer software specialist, "is when someone I've never heard of calls me out of the blue and tries to sell me something I didn't ask about. I want to shout into the phone, 'If I wanted to buy it, I'd have called you! Not the other way around.'"

Dealing with individuals like Al is what makes cold call selling such a challenge. Even after the initial sales are made to the names on your list, you've still got to generate repeat and new business. Thankfully there's an alternative that can "warm up" cold calls and make your job a whole lot easier: referrals.

Calling Your Referral Leads

Whether you're shopping for a new landscape company or someone to redesign your company's printed material, what's one of the first things you do? You ask for referrals from others you trust or admire.

Maybe your neighbor's lawn looks perennially green and weed-free—you want to know who maintains it because you want your yard to look the same way. So you call him, he gives you the number, and you place a call to inquire.

Or perhaps your company's marketing department is considering a redesign of an old brochure. They have a planning session and everyone brings examples of designs they think are effective.

A member of the team notices the XYZ Studio has designed one of the brochures. In her previous job, she used XYZ's services often and found them to be creative, reliable, and cost-efficient. After additional discussion, the marketing director says, "Let's give them a call and see what they can do for us," and the sales process begins.

If contacting a stranger is considered a "cold" call, then telephoning someone who has been referred to you as a possible new customer can definitely be described as "warm." This person comes to you with many defenses already down—and you feel the same way about him.

If he's been referred by a fellow businessman, he knows, for example, that you deliver on what you promise and that his associate's experience in doing business with you has been a positive one. You, on the other hand, know that he's already got an interest in your product or service because your friend—or present customer—has already indicated this is the case.

It's much less intimidating for both parties to begin the interaction because a sense of mutual trust already exists due to the third party you both know and respect. Some of the pressure is off and you find yourself talking in an almost friend-to-friend manner.

Old-fashioned word-of-mouth recommendations are worth their weight in gold. And there are many ways to make them happen. For example:

• An artist who creates personalized calligraphy for her customers establishes a warm, friendly atmosphere from the time the first telephone call is made until the artwork is delivered. "I put three business cards with every delivery and tell my customers it's their job to spread the word about my art," she says. "They're so pleased with the uniqueness and quality of my work, they're happy to do so. After twenty-three years, I still have many of the same customers who began by ordering for themselves and now they give my work as gifts to others."

• A do-it-yourself frame shop owner calls the local college's fine arts department and offers a 20 percent discount to students who bring their paintings in for framing. She also asks the college to exhibit her business cards and brochures at their next public exhibit. In return, she offers to hang and sell several of the students' best work in her store.

• An investment advisor thanks his current customer for referring prospective investors by giving him hard-to-come-by tickets to a hot new play or sporting event. "I want to give them something they'll really enjoy; something they'll want to tell their friends about—and ultimately I'm hoping those friends, after being spurred to remember that story, will ask my customer about my services and hopefully for my contact information."

Sometimes you'll need to take a direct approach. Early in the relationship, let it be known you are looking to expand your business. Ask your customer, "Will you consider referring two other associates that you think could benefit from an association such as the one we're developing?"

If they answer they don't know of anyone, help them jog their memory. Perhaps a vendor or another company in the office complex might have need of similar services. If your customer asks to remain anonymous in the referral, assure him you will honor the request—and then do so.

Don't be misled into thinking your customers will refer their friends and associates to you just because you stroke their ego or treat them to a free lunch or complimentary tickets to an event. They refer you because they believe your product or service will genuinely help. The ultimate influencing factors at work in successful referrals are the three "E's": excellent communication skills, effective problem solving, and extraordinary customer service—not the gifts.

Plant Seeds for Referrals

Customers are more likely to refer their friends and colleagues to you when they like you, your product, your service—especially your customer service. So how do you conduct business so as to ensure customer satisfaction—and set the stage for receiving referrals from them?

Ask yourself, "How would I want to be treated by a company?" and then go about the process of implementing some of your ideas into your efforts to increase your customer base. Obtaining new referrals starts by building upon your relationships with current customers.

Honesty, dependability, good service, fairness, and a positive and trusting attitude will keep your customers satisfied and returning their business to you. Most importantly, they'll be happy to spread the word and tell others about the good job you're doing for them. If they're the quiet type, as I've said before, you might have to just come right out and ask them to refer you to friends and business associates.

Keep in mind your customer might not be aware of everything your company offers. This is especially true for long-term customers. As with a lot of things, you can fall into a rut—they order the same thing season after season and everything's working just fine.

They don't ask about—and you don't tell them—about the new widget that's been added to your product lineup. Perhaps this new product will be of value to another department within their company or they themselves have a customer who can benefit from the new service.

Here are a couple of ways to update your current customers and their contacts:

- Spend some time brainstorming what makes your company different from your competitors. Boil it down to a short phrase and make it a priority to work it into the next conversation more than once the next time you contact your customer.

- Offer to give a workshop or seminar based on your new cutting-edge products or services that you've tailored toward the attendees' business. Tell your customers to invite fellow associates or friends who may also be interested in learning something new. Bring samples and leave-behinds (depending on your budget and the size of the group).

For example, if it's a morning seminar, include with your leave-behind sales material a discount coupon for the local coffee house—and, of course, attach your business card to it. Attach forms and a pen to several clipboards and pass them around to gather information during your presentation.

- Get more than names and phone numbers—ask why they've chosen to attend, what is their company's most pressing need, and other questions tailored to create a new association between what you offer and what they're looking to buy. You can also do a give-away, such as complimentary lunch for two at one of the best restaurants in town.

To enter, seminar attendees must put their business cards into a fish bowl. Just as the seminar ends, draw the lucky winner—and take the rest of the cards home with you! Your goal is to get the contact information of everyone who attends and then follow up with a phone call or handwritten note to introduce yourself one-on-one and get more information as soon as possible.

- Set up a file on your computer (index cards work just as well) with your prospective customer's information. Because you've already asked your current customer about his referral, you have an idea of what she is looking for and what is of interest to her. Note this in the file or on the card. As you go through newspapers and magazines or do Internet research, keep an eye out for news in your prospect's area of interest or expertise. Make a photocopy and send it to her with a short note that tells her indirectly you're thinking of her business needs and goals.

Keeping your name and contact information in the front of your customer's mind will help when she's asked for a referral by one of her associates. Although you think your current customers know all about your business, you might be surprised that the opposite is true.

Today's decision makers are inundated with information not only from outside sources but from within their company as well. It's easy to get tunnel vision and think only of solving immediate problems. Although you may enjoy a very satisfactory relationship with your customer, she is still concerned with your answer to one question—"What's in it for me/my friend whom I'm referring to you?"

Make asking for the referral easy by educating your customer as thoroughly as possible about your company so that he will keep your contact information close at hand. You might consider several different tactics to achieve this purpose.

Here are a few:

- Make your invoice a mini-advertisement. At the bottom of each form, add your strongest one-line sales feature, such as "Serving the Tri-State's Widget Needs for Over 25 Years" or "Our Commitment Is to Serve You with Complete Satisfaction."
- Use testimonials in your sales literature. For example, "I got a three-book deal from Random House and I credit this success to the how-to books I've purchased through the ABC Book Club."
- Simplify the way you describe your products and services. Avoid acronyms and phrases known only to certain businesses. Instead, use terms that everyone can understand.
- If the majority of your customers are located out-of-town, consider

getting an 800 number to make it more economical for them to call you with questions, problems—or new customers.

- Volunteer at an event that your customer supports. Make sure to wear a shirt with your company's logo and have plenty of business cards in your pocket should your customer introduce you around and the opportunity to network arises.

- Take advantage of being in the right place at the right time. For instance, you and your tennis partner at the club are talking about your prospective businesses after a match. He says to you, "Jim, I'm thinking of printing 10,000 inserts for our fall catalog. Do you know anyone who could handle that job?" That's a perfect referral opportunity, for yourself—if you're in the printing business—or to network one of your customers with your tennis partner.

- Consider asking your current customer if there are other departments within his organization that could use your products or services. If so, ask him if he'll make a personal introduction or write a letter of recommendation.

- Join your local chamber of commerce or other service organization such as the Rotary Club. Share your website address with your fellow members. You'll not only make new friends and learn more about the area in which you do business—you'll also increase the exposure of your company's goods and services to new customers.

- If you're looking to increase the number of in-town customers, consider taking out ads in community newspapers and magazines. Write a one- or two-page monthly or quarterly newsletter and mail it to the zip codes in which you'd like to add business. Don't make your recipients work to find your contact information—put that information in an obvious, easy-to-locate place.

- Offer an incentive that will help you and your prospective customer, such as adding a link to/from your website or propose an offer such as "Buy One/Get One for Half Price" with a qualified referral.

- Make sure you include your e-mail and website on your business card and your sales material. Make it easy for customers to contact you!

Sometimes referrals will come to you without much work on your part. Look at these as gifts, because most of the time you'll have to directly ask for referrals. Whether you take advantage of an off-hand remark like, "My sister is having the same problem with the widget machine in her office," or you plan your approach more formally, it is ultimately what you have to offer and how good the match is that will determine your future sales.

Referrals are a lot like networking. Reduced to its simplest form, you have a product or service that you believe in and someone else thinks highly enough about to want to share using it with his trusted friends and business associates. When someone recommends you, he is placing his own reputation on the line and trusting you to give his friend or associate the same quality service you are providing for his own organization.

Appendix: Resources

Contact Management Software

Act
1505 Pavilion Place
Norcross, GA 30093
Phone: 877-501-4496
Web: www.act.com

Goldmine
FrontRange Solutions
Phone: 800-776-7889
Web: www.frontrange.com

On Contact Software
Phone 800-886-0866
www.oncontact.com

Professional Organizations

Professional Society for Sales & Marketing Training
180 N. LaSalle Street, Suite 1822
Chicago, IL 60601

Phone: 312-551-0768
Fax: 312-551-0815
Web: www.smt.org

Direct Selling Association
1275 Pennsylvania Ave. NW, Ste. 800
Washington, DC 20004
Phone: 202-347-8866
Fax: 202-347-0055
E-mail: info@dsa.org
Web: www.dsa.org

Society for Marketing Professional Services
99 Canal Center Plaza, Suite 330
Alexandria, VA 22314
Phone: 800-292-7677
Fax: 703-549-2498
E-mail: info@smps.org
Web: www.smps.org

Websites

www.mgtclass.mgt.unm.edu/MIDS/Sacco/Chapter%2021/Sales%20and%20
Marketing%20Resources.doc

Lists close to 60 sales/marketing related books, 30 magazines, 13 national professional associations, and 18 local professional associations.

www.sohocentralusa.com/salesmktg.htm

The Resource Channel Sales & Marketing Resources website features information, books, and resources on sales and marketing.

www.massbedrock.org/catalog/catalog.cfm?SUB1 = 120&
CFNoCache = TRUE&offset = 1 (the general site is www.massbedrock.org)

MassBedrock (Massachusetts Business and Economic Development

Reference Online Center for Knowledge) is a service of the University of Massachusetts Libraries.

www.ebusinesstutor.com/staticpages/index.php/resources
　　Mainly geared toward e-marketing.

www.bestofsales.com/

Sales Books

Beckwith, Harry. *Selling the Invisible*. Warner Books, 1997.

Bettger, Frank. *How I Raised Myself from Failure to Success in Selling*. Prentice Hall, 1970.

Cates, Bill. *Unlimited Referrals*. Thunder Hill Press, 1996.

Crandall, Rick (Editor). *Celebrate Selling the Consultative-Relationship Way*. Select Press, 1998.

Crosby, John. *Managing the Big Sale*. NTC Business Books, 1996.

Daley, Kevin. *Socratic Selling*. Irwin, 1996.

Farber, Barry. *Sales Secrets from Your Customers*. Career Press, 1995.

——. *State of the Art Selling*. Career Press, 1994.

——. *Superstar Sales Secrets*. Career Press, 1995.

Gerson, Richard. *Winning the Inner Game of Selling*. Crisp Publications, 1999.

Girard, Joe. *How to Close Every Sale*. Warner Books, 1989.

Gschwandtner, Gerhard. *Selling Power's Best*. Personal Selling Power, 1996.

Hanan, Mack. *Consultative Selling, Seventh Edition*. AMACOM, 2004.

——, James Cribbin, and Jack Donis. *Systems Selling Strategies*. AMACOM, 1978.

Hopkins, Tom. *Selling for Dummies*. Wiley Publishing, 2001.

Johnson, Spencer. *The One-Minute Salesperson*. Avon, 1984.

Kalench, John. *17 Secrets of Master Prospectors*. MIM Publications, 1994.

Kennedy, Dan. *No B.S. Sales Success*. Self-Counsel Press, 1984.

Maltz, Maxwell. *Zero-Resistance Selling*. Prentice Hall, 1998.

Miller, Robert, Stephen Heiman, and Tad Tuleja. *Successful Large Account Management.* Warner Books, 1991.

———. *The New Strategic Selling.* Warner Books, 1998.

Parinello, Anthony. *Dynamic Selling.* Alpha, 1998.

———. *Selling to VITO.* Adams Media, 1999.

Pickens, James. *More Art of Closing Any Deal.* Shapolsky, 1991.

Raphel, Murray, and Neil Raphel. *Tough Selling for Tough Times.* Raphel Publishing, 1992.

Schiffman, Stephan. *Cold Calling Techniques. Adams Media, 1999.*

———. *The 25 Most Common Sales Mistakes.* Bob Adams, 1990.

Shook, Robert. *Ten Greatest Salespersons.* Harper & Row, 1978.

St. Lawrence, Michael, and Steve Johnson. *If You're Not Out Selling You're Being Outsold.* John Wiley & Sons, 1998.

Sales Training Firms

Adrian Miller
Adrian Miller Direct Marketing
43 Park Ave.
Port Washington, NY 11050
Phone: 516-767-9288
Fax: 516-767-0702
Web: www.adrianmiller.com

Paul Karasik
The Business Institute
3416 Alma Avenue
Manhattan Beach, CA 90266-3329
Phone: 310-545-4994
Fax: 310-545-2346
E-mail: paul@paulkarasik.com
Web: www.paulkarasik.com

Caliper
506 Carnegie Center, #300

Princeton, NJ 08540
Phone: 609-524-1200
Web: www.calipercorp.com

Mr. Bill Caskey
Caskey Achievement Strategies
10333 N. Meridian Street, Suite 101
Indianapolis, IN 46290-1074
Phone: 317-575-0057
Fax: 317-575-0168
bcaskey@caskeytraining.com

D.E.I. Management Group, Inc.
888 Seventh Avenue, 9th Floor
New York, NY 10106
Phone: 800-224-2140
Fax: 212-245-7897

Integrity Systems
1850 North Central Avenue, Suite 100
Phoenix, AZ 85004-4527
Phone: 800-896-9090
Fax: 602-253-9600
Web: www.integritysystems.com

Richardson
Phone: 800-526-1650
Web: www.richardson.com

Thomas M. Begg
SoftSell PitBull
Glen Rock, NJ
Phone: 201-251-1822

tombegg@softsellpitbull.com
www.softsellpitbull.com

Periodicals

Selling Power magazine
Subscription Department
P.O. Box 5467
Fredericksburg, VA 22403-9980
Phone: 800-752-7355
Web: www.sellingpower.com

Index

About the Author

Bob Bly is an independent copywriter, consultant, and seminar leader with twenty-five years of experience in writing sales scripts, lead-generating sales letters, sales presentations, e-mail marketing campaigns, websites, and other sales prospecting materials. He also teaches selling skills classes through his training company, the Center for Technical Communication.

Bob has written sales copy for over 100 customers, including Network Solutions, ITT Fluid Technology, Medical Economics, Intuit, Business & Legal Reports, and Brooklyn Union Gas. Awards include a Gold Echo from the Direct Marketing Association, an IMMY from the Information Industry Association, two Southstar Awards, an American Corporate Identity Award of Excellence, and the Standard of Excellence award from the Web Marketing Association.

Bob is the author of more than sixty books, including *The Complete Idiot's Guide to Direct Marketing* (Alpha Books), *Selling Your Services* (Henry Holt & Co.), and *Successful Telephone Selling* (Henry Holt & Co.).

His monthly e-zine on sales and marketing, *The Direct Response Letter*, reaches over 50,000 subscribers. His website, www.bly.com, gets over 4,000 hits monthly—without advertising or search engine optimization.

Bob's articles have appeared in numerous publications, such as *Amtrak*

Express, Cosmopolitan, Successful Meetings, Inside Direct Mail, and *Bits & Pieces for Salespeople,* of which he was formerly editor. He has regular columns on sales and marketing in five publications: *Early to Rise, DM News, Writer's Digest, Internet Media Review,* and *Subscription Marketing.*

Bob has presented sales and marketing seminars for such groups as the U.S. Army, Independent Laboratory Distributors Association, IBM, Thoroughbred Software, Whirlpool, and the American Marketing Association. He also taught marketing at New York University.

Prior to becoming an independent copywriter, trainer, and consultant, Bob was communications manager for Koch Engineering, a manufacturer of process equipment. He has also worked as a marketing communications writer for Westinghouse Defense.

Bob Bly holds a B.S. in chemical engineering from the University of Rochester and has been trained as a Certified Novell Administrator (CNA). He is a member of the American Institute of Chemical Engineers, Newsletter and Electronic Publishers Association, and the Business Marketing Association.